Greater than the Sum
of Its Parts?

International
Peace Academy

Greater than the Sum of Its Parts?

Assessing "Whole of Government" Approaches to Fragile States

Stewart Patrick   **Kaysie Brown**

International Peace Academy, 777 United Nations Plaza, New York, NY 10017
www.ipacademy.org
© 2007 by International Peace Academy
All rights reserved. Published 2007.

International Peace Academy (IPA) is an independent international institution dedicated to promoting the prevention and settlement of armed conflicts between and within states through policy research and development.

The views expressed in this publication represent those of the authors and not necessarily those of IPA. IPA welcomes consideration of a wide range of perspectives in the pursuit of a well-informed debate on critical policies and issues in international affairs.

ISBN: 0-937722-98-7
ISBN-13: 978-0-937722-98-5

Cover design by Anne Maroon, www.annemaroon.com
Text design by Andrew Nofsinger with Adam Lupel, www.andrewnofsinger.com

CONTENTS

Foreword

Terje Rød-Larsen

President, International Peace Academy

The International Peace Academy is pleased to publish *Greater than the Sum of Its Parts?—Assessing "Whole of Government" Approaches to Fragile States*, by Stewart Patrick and Kaysie Brown. This timely book provides the first independent, comparative assessment of recent efforts by individual donor governments to integrate their defense, diplomatic, development, and other policies in engaging weak, failing, and war-torn countries in the developing world. The impetus for this trend is clear: Fragile states are at once a major development challenge and a leading source of transnational threats to global security. Through sometimes painful experience, donors have also come to recognize that the security, governance, and development challenges of these troubled countries are highly interconnected. To advance reform, prevent state failure, and promote peace and recovery in war-torn states, donors need to employ the entire panoply of policy instruments at their disposal. In short, stove-piped policy responses are "out," integrated approaches are "in."

At the same time, this rhetorical commitment to "whole of government" approaches conceals fundamental dilemmas and difficult choices in the quest for policy coherence. As this book makes clear, individual donor governments are still struggling to develop a strategic approach to state fragility; to define the goals of their national policies; to agree on departmental divisions of labor and coordination mechanisms; to mobilize adequate resources to meet the challenge of fragile states; to harmonize their approaches with other donors; to align their efforts with host governments; and to monitor and evaluate the impact of their policy interventions.

This book explores the challenges of policy coherence in

fragile states by analyzing the recent experiences of seven leading donors: the United Kingdom, the United States, Canada, Australia, Germany, France, and Sweden. These case studies underscore the tensions inherent in efforts to reconcile the priorities and time frames of foreign, defense, and development ministries—and the difficulty of achieving "joined-up" responses that can simultaneously address goals of poverty alleviation, accountable governance, stability and security in fragile states. The book provides an incisive complement to the recently released OECD/DAC report on whole of government approaches. It candidly addresses shortcomings in existing donor strategies, mechanisms, and arrangements, while also calling attention to promising institutional developments.

This volume is aimed at a wide audience. It is of clear interest to the development community, which has long been preoccupied with the issue of policy coherence and the challenges of aid effectiveness in difficult environments. But it will also be of interest to the broader foreign policy and national security communities, which are increasingly preoccupied with the challenges of building effective states in some of the most volatile and conflict-ridden parts of the world. We hope that this book injects new ideas and a sober realism into ongoing discussions about how to bridge gaps among the development, defense, and diplomatic communities.

The research and publication of this report would not have been possible without generous support provided by the Carnegie Corporation of New York and IPA's core funders, to all of whom we remain deeply grateful.

Acknowledgments

The report is based in part on scores of off-the-record interviews with officials in donor ministries, who graciously agreed to speak to the authors at length, in candid terms, on the performance of their agencies and governments. We are enormously grateful to these colleagues in the United Kingdom (Cabinet Office, Ministry of Defense, Foreign and Commonwealth Office, Department for International Development, and Post-Conflict Reconstruction Unit); the United States (National Security Council, State Department, US Agency for International Development, Department of Defense, Treasury Department, and National Intelligence Council); Canada (Privy Council Office, Canadian International Development Agency, Ministry of Defense, and Department for Foreign Affairs and International Trade); Australia (Australian Agency for International Development, Australian Federal Police, Department of Foreign Affairs and Trade, the International Deployment Group, and the Department of Defense); Germany (Foreign Office, Ministry of Defense, Federal Ministry of Economic Cooperation and Development, German Technical Cooperation, and Center for International Peace Operations); France (Agence Française de Développement, Secretariat General de la Defense Nationale, Ministère des Affaires Étrangeres, and Ministère de la Défense Nationale); and Sweden (Swedish International Development Agency, Foreign Ministry, and Ministry of Defense). Needless to say, none of the views or judgments contained in this report should be taken as any indication of private sentiment or official policy on the part of our interlocutors.

The authors also benefited from conversations with multiple independent scholars, experts, and other individuals. We thank in particular Luc van de Goor of the Netherlands Institute of International Relations (Clingendael), who coordinated a parallel study for the OECD/DAC on "Whole of Government Approaches to Fragile States," the conclusions of which mirror some of our own findings. We also benefited from the wise counsel of Nicole Ball of the Center for International Policy; Mariano

Aguirre of the Fondaçion para las Relaçiones Internacionales y el Diálogo Exterior in Madrid; Roland Paris of the University of Ottawa; Karim Morcos of the OECD/DAC Secretariat; Nick Mabey of Third Generation Environmentalism; Clare Lockhart of the Overseas Development Institute; Dylan Hendrickson of Kings College, London; and Ulrich Schneckener and Stefan Mair of the German Institute for International and Security Affairs.

The authors are grateful to IPA President Terje Rød-Larsen and Vice President Elizabeth Cousens for supporting this effort. We thank Vanessa Wyeth of IPA for her steadfast assistance in bringing this project to fruition, and Adam Lupel for supervising the production of this volume.

Finally, we express our sincere gratitude to Nancy Birdsall, President of the Center for Global Development, and CGD Vice-President Dennis de Tray for supporting our research on more effective donor responses to fragile states.

Acronyms

AA	Auswärtiges Amt (German Foreign Office)
ACPP	Africa Conflict Prevention Pool (UK)
AFD	Agence Française de Développement (France)
AFP	Australian Federal Police
AU	African Union
AusAID	Australian Agency for International Development
BMZ	Federal Ministry for Economic Cooperation and Development (Germany)
CGD	Center for Global Development
CHASE	Conflict, Humanitarian and Security Department (UK)
CICID	Interministerial Committee for International Cooperation and Development (France)
CDPF	Country Development Programming Framework (Canada)
CIDA	Canadian International Development Agency
CIG	Conflict Issues Group (UK)
CPIA	Country Policy and Institutional Assessment
CPS	Civilian Police Service (Germany)
CRI	Countries at Risk of Instability
CSR	Comprehensive Spending Review (UK)
DAC	Development Assistance Committee (OECD)
DCP	Document Cadre Partenariat (France)
DDR	Disarmament, Demobilization and Reintegration
DFA	Director of Foreign Assistance (US)
DFAT	Department of Foreign Affairs and Trade (Australia)
DFAIT	Department of Foreign Affairs and International Trade (Canada)
DFID	Department for International Development (UK)
DGCID	Direction Général de la Cooperation Internationale au Développement (France)
DND	Department of National Defense (Canada)
DoD	Department of Defense (US)
ESS	European Security Strategy
FANS	Foreign Affairs and National Security Committee (Canada)
FRG	Federal Republic of Germany
FCO	Foreign and Commonwealth Office (UK)
GCPP	Global Conflict Prevention Pool (UK)
GPSF	Global Peace and Security Fund (Canada)
GTZ	Deutsche Gesellschaft für Technische Zusammenarbeit (German Technical Cooperation)
HMG	Her Majesty's Government (UK)
IDA	International Development Association

IDC	Interdepartmental Committee (Australia)
IDG	International Deployment Group (Australia)
IJSD	Integrated Justice Sector Development (UK)
IPA	International Peace Academy
IPS	International Policy Statement (Canada)
ISAF	International Security Assistance Force
JIC	Joint Intelligence Committee (UK)
MAE	Ministère des Affaires Étrangeres (France)
MDGs	Millennium Development Goals
MCA	Millennium Challenge Account (US)
MINEFI	Ministry of Economic Affairs, Finance and Industry (France)
MoD	Ministry of Defense
MoI	Ministry of the Interior (Germany)
NSPD	National Security Presidential Directive (US)
NEPAD	New Partnership for Africa's Development
NIC	National Intelligence Council (US)
NSC	National Security Council (US)
OECD	Organization for Economic Cooperation and Development
ODA	Official Development Assistance
ODE	Office of Development Effectiveness (Australia)
OEF	Operation Enduring Freedom
OMA	Office of Military Affairs (US)
PCO	Privy Council Office (Canada)
PCRU	Post-Conflict Reconstruction Unit (UK)
PEPFAR	President's Emergency Plan for AIDS Relief (US)
PMSU	Prime Minister's Strategy Unit
PNG	Papua New Guinea
PRT	Provincial Reconstruction Team
PSA	Public Service Agreement (UK)
PSEP	Department of Public Safety and Emergency Preparedness (Canada)
RAMSI	Regional Assistance Mission to Solomon Islands
RECAMP	Renforcement des Capacités Africaines de Maintien de la Paix
RCMP	Royal Canadian Mounted Police
S/CRS	Office of the Coordinator of Reconstruction and Stabilization (US)
SGDN	Secretariat General de La Defense Nationale (France)
SIDA	Swedish International Development Agency
SSR	Security sector reform
START	Stabilization and Reconstruction Task Force (Canada)
USAID	United States Agency for International Development
WMD	Weapons of mass destruction
ZIF	Center for International Peace Operations (Germany)
ZSP	Zone de Priorité Solidaire (France)

Introduction

Fragile states represent both the crux of today's development challenge and an increasing source of potential threats to global security.[1] Experience suggests that efforts to bolster, reform, or reconstruct such countries must simultaneously address security and stability, good governance, and development needs. To do so effectively, donors must draw on a wide range of capabilities and instruments spanning traditionally independent spheres of diplomacy, development, and defense (the 3Ds), as well as trade, finance, intelligence, and others. Moreover, these elements of engagement should be consciously aligned so as to be mutually reinforcing.

The current policy attention to weak and failing states reflects the confluence of two principal sets of concerns related to development and security. First, the international development community, including the bilateral donors of the OECD, the World Bank, and UN agencies, has come to recognize that standard development principles and practice are often of limited utility in engaging a subset of poorly performing developing countries that lack either the political commitment or the practical capacity to deliver basic services and pro-poor policies. Countries such as Afghanistan, Haiti, Liberia, and Yemen tend to suffer from low or negative levels of development and poor governance, and (in many cases) are mired in violent conflict. According to the UK's Department for International Development (DFID), nearly one-third of aid recipients live in fragile states.[2] Such states often receive less assistance than better performing developing countries, reinforcing their marginalization and contributing to the phenomenon of "aid orphans."[3] The World Bank and OECD donors have struggled to find effective ways to engage such "difficult partners."[4]

At the same time, national security officials in donor capitals have come to regard weak and failing states as potential dangers to international peace and security (to say nothing of the security of their inhabitants), apt to generate a range of negative "spillover" effects in the form of transnational terrorism, organized crime, weapons proliferation, global pandemics, environmental degradation, and the spread of violent conflict. This new threat perception was magnified by the attacks on the United States of September 11, 2001, in which terrorists operating from the world's second poorest country inflicted grievous damage on the world's most powerful state. To many in the international community, the attacks showed that fragile and failing states represent the weakest link in global collective security.

This sentiment was ratified at the UN World Summit in September 2005, which endorsed an outcome document designed to strengthen both the multilateral architecture and the sovereign capacities of all states to address today's global threats.[5] At a national level, the difficulties encountered in stabilizing and reconstructing war-torn countries, including Afghanistan, Iraq, Sudan, and other states, have led donor governments to explore integrated approaches to post-conflict operations (several of which are discussed in this book). This effort has been mirrored at the multilateral level by the creation of the UN Peacebuilding Commission in early 2006.

In response to these concerns, there has been increased understanding within the donor community that, for development actors, the challenge of fragile states implies not only *doing things differently* but also *doing different things*.[6] First, standard development practice, in everything from education to health care assistance, needs to be adapted to the realities of state fragility, which typically implies the lack of a capable and/or legitimate state. Second, effective donor responses in fragile environments may imply doing things outside traditional development expertise, such as civilian policing and military reform. This may involve collaboration between development agencies with non-development ministries that are more experienced (as well as mandated) to address these tasks, such as in the disarmament of former combatants.

Because building effective states in the developing world requires addressing both development and security concerns, there is growing recognition that development agencies must "join up" with other departments with comparative advantages and unique capabilities, particularly diplomatic and defense ministries. Recently, several OECD governments have launched "whole of government" approaches in poorly performing countries, for example, by drafting government or agency-wide fragile states strategies, creating new offices to address conflict prevention or reconstruction, and allowing for different types of funding arrangements so as to promote greater collaboration among ministries. In response to these trends, in January 2005, the OECD/DAC held a Senior Level Forum on Fragile States. That gathering generated a set of *Principles for Good International Engagement in Fragile States*. Among other things, the document calls for greater coherence between donor government agencies to promote a "whole of government approach, involving those responsible for security, political and economic affairs, as well as those responsible for development aid and humanitarian assistance."[7] In late 2005, the newly formed Fragile States Group of the OECD/DAC launched its own dedicated work stream, under the leadership of Australia and France, aiming to provide guidance to donors on how to improve whole of government approaches in fragile states.[8] Indeed, the challenge of fragile states is now squarely on the donor community's agenda.

This study examines efforts to promote policy coherence toward fragile states by seven donor governments: the United Kingdom, the United States, Canada, Australia, France, Germany, and Sweden. It reflects extensive consultations with officials of these governments, as well as discussions with knowledgeable outside observers in academia and think tanks. In looking at each country, we hoped to glean insights into the motivations, assumptions, and rationales behind this new strategic reorientation, as well as the challenges of reconciling mandates and creating effective coordination mechanisms. Beyond a better understanding of the conceptual issues and motivations of the donor community, this study attempts to catalog the practical strides made in advancing policy coherence, the resources and instruments available to implement joined-up approaches, and the early implications of any pilot projects.

A Note on Fragility

A major obstacle to crafting more integrated approaches to fragile states is the lack of common understanding about what "fragility" actually means. Beyond the general recognition that fragile states are overwhelmingly poor and exhibit severe sovereignty deficiencies, there is little international consensus about how to define and measure the phenomenon, and about which countries merit the label. At the official level, Britain's Department for International Development (DFID) has produced a list of forty-six "fragile" states, defined as poor countries unable or unwilling to use domestic and international resources effectively for the purpose of poverty reduction.[10] The World Bank has its own classification, labeling twenty-five very poor, troubled countries as "low income countries under stress," as determined by scores on the Bank's Country Policy and Institutional Assessments.[11] The US Agency for International Development (USAID), meanwhile, defines fragile states as those lacking the capacity and legitimacy to deliver public goods in the political, economic, security, and social spheres, and it has proposed thirty-three indicators to measure state performance in each of these four areas.[12]

These official efforts have been complemented by independent efforts to define and measure state fragility and susceptibility to failure. The CIA-supported *Political Instability Task Force* has an impressive track record of predicting state failure, which it defines as a "severe internal political crisis."[13] The report of the *Commission on Weak States and US National Security* classifies fifty to sixty countries as "weak," based on their failure to provide security, social welfare, and legitimate institutions.[14] The Fund for Peace's *Failed States Index* grades states according to their susceptibility to political instability, focusing primarily on the risk of violence.[15] A recent project of Carleton University, the *Country Indicators for Foreign Policy*, measures the state's ability to provide basic governance across a wide range of spheres.[16] Ashraf Ghani, Clare Lockhart, and Michael Carnahan have proposed a sovereignty index to measure state strength, focused heavily on financial and economic components of state function.[17] Finally, Stewart Patrick of the Center for Global Development and Susan Rice of the Brookings Institution have recently completed an *Index of State Weakness in the Developing World*, which rates all developing and transitional countries—143 in all—according to their performance in four dimensions of state function: political, security, economic, and social welfare.[18]

Of course, measuring state strength does not say enough about the current circumstances and trajectory of a country, nor about the prospects for constructive policy dialogue between donors and the governing regime. One might distinguish among several categories of weak states, each of which presents distinctive challenges and require differentiated approaches. These may include: endemically weak states that are not at a major risk of conflict but are nonetheless characterized by low growth, anemic institutions, and patrimonial systems of political leadership; resource-rich poor performers, which are often oil-rich countries led by corrupt, autocratic regimes; deteriorating countries, or those that suffer a marked decline in institutional performance with an increased risk of violence or state collapse; countries in the throes of crises, either in the form of prolonged political impasse or violence; post-conflict states; brittle dictatorships; and reform-minded governments. These different scenarios, along with the degree to which a government actually has either the capacity or the will to deliver the goods associated with effective statehood, will inevitably entail different levels and forms of engagement by donor governments.

The focus of "policy coherence," as the term is used in this book, is primarily on the roles of three main sets of donor actors focusing on fragile state challenges: development ministries, foreign ministries, and defense ministries, often referred to as the 3Ds. We recognize that comprehensive policy coherence may also involve other departments and agencies, including finance, intelligence, interior, and trade ministries, and where these agencies have been heavily involved, we address their role. The analysis here focuses primarily on policy advancements and institutional innovations that have taken place in state capitals.[9] As the report points out, this trend toward integrated national efforts carries significant potential for synergies among the various departments, and for dealing with the interdependent challenges they face. At the same time, individual donors are only beginning to navigate the trade-offs and tensions inherent in attempting to reconcile and harmonize their distinct mandates, objectives, and time lines.

A Preview of the Findings and Recommendations

Overall, as elaborated in our Conclusion, we find that while laudable strides have been made among select countries, the concept of state "fragility" remains contested and controversial even within and among the leading donor governments we examine here. There is little common understanding among agencies about what constitutes a fragile state, much less a common, government-wide strategic vision on priority objectives in weak and failed states. Individual governments often avoid frank debate over the goals of policy coherence in fragile states, in part because they are reluctant to confront the divergent motivations for their efforts. Integrated country strategies, based on joint country assessments and planning, exist more in theory than in practice. The development community, in particular, remains deeply ambivalent about the quest for policy coherence. On the one hand, integrated approaches may garner increased attention and resources for fragile states; on the other, they may subordinate the goal of poverty alleviation to short-term security imperatives. We also find a dearth of strong coordinating entities and dedicated funding streams to address the specific challenges of engaging fragile states. Experience suggests that standing inter-agency units can help create a focal point for cross-departmental collaboration within donor governments, but they are also vulnerable to debilitating weaknesses, particularly when they lack bureaucratic heft and dedicated resources. Funding shortfalls remain a major constraint to greater collaboration of agencies working in fragile states, and while integrated funding mechanisms can encourage policy coherence, pooled funds by themselves cannot compensate for disagreement on ends.

Where advances have been made in whole of government approaches toward fragile states, these have often been in responding to crisis and assisting post-conflict recovery, as opposed to preventing state failure and violent conflict to begin with. Notwithstanding its higher profile, post-conflict response still suffers from multiple deficiencies, most notably in the failure of donor states to create adequate civilian capacity to address the quintessentially "civilian" activities inherent in reconstructing war-torn societies, particularly in the realms of the rule of law, governance, and economic recovery. Furthermore, donors are just beginning to develop common doctrine between civilian and military actors, integrated planning mechanisms, and joint training for post-conflict operations, and they have been slow to create standing civilian operational capacities. Joint monitoring and early warning of potential crisis countries continue to meet bureaucratic resistance, given the divergent approaches and priorities of relevant agencies. Finally, for all the talk about the importance of joined-up approaches in headquarters, donor governments overwhelmingly do not share a common vision of "jointness" in the field.

In order to make recognizable progress in stabilizing and reforming fragile states, donor governments will have to embrace some painful but necessary changes in the way they engage the world's most troubled countries. As a first step, donors must commit to open and candid dialogue, both internally among their national agencies and with other donor governments, about how to balance the multiple goals and objectives involved in working in fragile states, with an eye on how best to advance long-term institution-building. Second, donors should develop a unified country strategy for each fragile state in which they plan to engage. This common country strategy should drive a comprehensive assistance strategy, with flexibility to adapt nimbly to changing circumstances. A starting point for policy coherence toward fragile states must be an institutionalized, integrated system for early warning and assessment, as well as the development of ways to evaluate the impact of donor interventions on state fragility. Third, high-level political commitment, guidance, and departmental leadership are imperative to advance this agenda within donor governments. Without buy-in at senior levels, even well intentioned coordinating units or mechanisms can be sidelined and proven ineffective. Such high-level endorsement should be reinforced by meaningful professional incentives that reward "jointness" across ministries.

Fourth, money matters. Donor governments should devote a greater share of foreign assistance to fragile states, as well as create common pools to stimulate cross-departmental collaboration. Access by agencies to pooled funding should be contingent on genuine agreement on strategic priorities and joint oversight of implementation. Donors should also make full use of the current OECD/DAC rules concerning the uses of Official Development Assistance (ODA), and consider expanding ODA eligibility criteria for security sector reform activities. In post-conflict contexts, especially, there is no substitute for standing contingency funds that permit rapid crisis response. Donors must also deepen tentative efforts to create standing civilian capabilities for rapid deployment to the field. Finally, and importantly, the development of integrated fragile state policies within donor governments must not preclude harmonization of international efforts and alignment with host government priorities.

Taking these steps should greatly improve the ability of donor governments, individually and collectively, to assist fragile states struggling to avoid failure and to rebuild in the wake of war. In the end, of course, the fate of fragile states will be shaped primarily by the commitment and capacities of their own governments and citizens. By getting their own house in order, however, donor governments may be able to contribute to these efforts.

Chapter One

The United Kingdom

Overview

Among donor countries, the United Kingdom has been at the forefront of conceiving and adopting integrated policy responses to weak and failing states. Its innovations include new methodologies for cross-Whitehall assessments of instability and conflict, the use of common resource "pools" to encourage interdepartmental collaboration in conflict prevention and mitigation, and a specialized post-conflict unit to foster civilian-military coordination in responding to war-torn countries. Cross-Whitehall skills and experience are increasingly rewarded professionally within the UK government. The UK's relative progress reflects early recognition within Britain of the unique development and security challenges posed by poorly performing, unstable, and conflict-ridden countries, as well as the explicit commitment by Prime Minister Tony Blair to foster "whole of government" approaches to daunting foreign policy challenges. It also testifies to the strength and dynamism of the Department for International Development (DFID), as a fully fledged cabinet agency possessing significant resources and the liberty to pursue innovative approaches to the linkages between development, governance, and security. The UK's interest in policy coherence was reinforced by the 2005 *Report of the Commission for Africa*, sponsored by the prime minister.[19]

Despite these pioneering conceptual and institutional innovations, the UK's performance in designing and implementing coherent, integrated strategies toward fragile states continues to fall short of its aspirations. Effective cross-Whitehall approaches remain elusive, hampered not only by conflicting mandates and cultures, but also by the lack of underlying consensus among departments on national objectives and the means to achieve them. The UK's record suggests that improved communication, common resource pools, and coordination mechanisms can improve policy response, but are no substitute for a clear, agreed-upon strategic framework reflecting common priorities.

Origins and Motivations

In contrast to the United States, where concern over weak and failing states was marginal prior to 9/11, British preoccupation with fragile states antedates the "global war on terrorism." It originated in experiences in Sierra Leone and other African countries during the 1990s, which persuaded DFID, in particular, that violent conflict posed a significant obstacle to development.[20] DFID's White Paper of 2000, *Eliminating World Poverty: Making Globalization Work for the Poor*, made this connection explicit, identifying personal security as prerequisite for sustainable livelihoods. In 2001, Clare Short, the first secretary of state for DFID, inspired the creation of the interdepartmental Africa Conflict Prevention Pool (ACPP), and subsequently the Global Conflict Prevention Pool (GCPP), intended to facilitate common funding and interdepartmental collaboration on critical conflict mitigation activities like disarmament, demobilization, and reintegration (DDR), and security sector reform (SSR), that fall outside conventional ODA.

Since 9/11, a broader set of foreign policy and development considerations have deepened the UK's interest in fragile and conflict-ridden states, widely perceived to pose myriad dangers to the country's security, economic, and humanitarian interests. The Ministry of Defence (MoD) and the Foreign and Commonwealth Office (FCO), in particular, regard such nations as potential havens for terrorism and possible sources of regional instability and energy insecurity. The Home Office, likewise, worries about their domestic implications for refugee flows and organized crime.

DFID, meanwhile, views them as the hard core of the development challenge, one that cannot be ignored despite the growing focus on "good performers," or countries that have achieved notable results in improving governance and economic growth. The Prime Minister's Strategy Unit (PMSU) crystallized these multiple concerns in an influential 2004 report, *Investing in Prevention: An International Strategy to Manage Risks of Instability and Improve Crisis Response*. It depicted effective states as the answer to security, poverty alleviation, and good governance in the developing world, and it called for a new whole of government strategy to engage Countries at Risk of Instability (CRI).[21] *Investing in Prevention* proposed a sophisticated methodology to assess instability in any given country, and a strategic planning process to design comprehensive interventions involving all relevant UK and international actors.[22] As we will see below, the CRI methodology has not been fully internalized or exploited by the UK government.

Finally, the wars in Afghanistan and Iraq exposed shortcomings in the UK's capacity to help stabilize and reconstruct post-conflict countries (particularly during active insurgency), and generated intense interdepartmental disputes over the desirable relative roles of the MoD, the FCO, and DFID in designing and implementing such operations. In response, the government, in summer 2004, created the Post-Conflict Reconstruction Unit (PCRU), intended to improve the strategic and operational coherence of the UK's stabilization efforts and to develop a deployable civilian force whose expertise and skill sets would complement—and in some cases replace—those of UK troops. After a difficult gestation and birth, the PCRU is attempting to find its feet within the UK bureaucracy.

A Common Strategic Vision?

Although the entire UK government is keenly interested in the implications of weak, failing, and unstable states in the developing world, the lens through which each UK department views such countries reflects its unique institutional mandate as a developmental, diplomatic, or defense actor. Even when departments agree on the diagnosis, the courses of treatment they prescribe may be mutually incompatible. For all the whole of government rhetoric, one UK official noted, "There is not a lot of coherence here." The UK experience suggests that *a joined-up approach to fragile states depends on a prior whole of government consensus on what constitutes a "fragile state."*

Indeed, within the UK government, the concept of "fragility" is fully embraced only within DFID, to describe a class of troubled, often badly governed, poor countries that risk being left behind by the donor community's focus on good performers. As DFID explains in its January 2005 strategy document, *Why We Need to Work More Effectively in Fragile States*, a fragile state is one "where the government cannot or will not deliver core functions to the majority of its people, including the poor."[23] DFID defines fragile states as those countries that (i) are eligible for funds from the World Bank's International Development Association (IDA) window and (ii) rank within the lowest two quintiles on the World Bank's Country Policy and Institutional Assessments (CPIA). It estimates that some forty-six nations with approximately 870 million inhabitants fall into this category.

For DFID, the primary questions in settings where capacity and commitment are lacking are how foreign assistance can be made more effective and how non-development instruments can be integrated in building sound institutions and, importantly, in alleviating poverty. The goal of policy coherence is to bring the unique resources and skills of other departments to bear in addressing security and governance obstacles to development in fragile states. Significantly, DFID treats "security" first and foremost from the perspective of the inhabitants of partner countries themselves, rather than that of UK citizens. While an integrated response may have ancillary benefits for UK national security, its primary goal is to ensure sufficient physical and human security for local individuals and communities to pursue sustainable livelihoods and make progress toward the Millennium Development Goals (MDGs).

The FCO and the MoD share neither DFID's concept of fragility nor its focus on poverty alleviation. They tend to be more fixated on the risk of political instability and violent conflict, and on its potential implications for UK national interests, including possible spillover effects of state failure like transnational terrorism and crime, weapons proliferation, interruption of energy supplies, and the undermining of regional allies. As an indication of these divergent perspectives, in recent years the MoD has periodically pressed DFID to consider Saudi Arabia as a "fragile" state—and to begin programs in that country. DFID has resisted, on the grounds that Saudi Arabia is not fragile, that it is unclear what DFID would do there, and that the Saudis have adequate domestic resources to address their own internal development.[24]

As this example suggests, DFID often faces pressure to devote a greater share of its considerable resources (which exceed the FCO's aid budget by a factor of nine to one) to countries and purposes deemed critical to UK security interests. Unlike aid agencies in many donor countries, however, DFID is well positioned to rebuff these efforts. Besides being a full cabinet department, DFID is governed by the International Development Act, which mandates that its funds be spent "to support sustainable development." This gives the secretary of state for development near total discretion over the use of those funds—much to the frustration of the FCO and the MoD, which believe that DFID hides behind the act to resist justifiable aid reallocations to strategic partners for security purposes. DFID's Public Service Agreement (PSA) with the Treasury provides an additional constraint on the diversion of DFID resources, by mandating that 90 percent of the department's budget be spent on low-income countries—effectively restricting the lion's share of DFID's aid to the poorest regions of Africa and Asia.

For DFID, a whole of government approach provides a means to bring other levers of UK policy—as well as additional non-ODA funds—to bear in fulfilling certain functions (such as security sector reform) that are critical to poverty alleviation and long-term development, but for which it has neither the expertise nor the resources. It can also help to ensure the harmonization and sequencing of developmental, military, and political processes. At the same time, DFID has reservations about diluting its poverty reduction mandate, and is wary of seeing its own resources diverted to security goals. For example, the department is still getting around to the idea that terrorism is relevant to its work, even though its presence can pose a grave threat to development in countries like Bangladesh or Kenya (where attacks have injured the tourism industry). DFID is also wary about broadening the definition of ODA, lest its funds be diverted to post-conflict police building or peacekeeping, for example. While the July 2006 DFID White Paper has reaffirmed the centrality of fragile states for the department's work, even within DFID there are tensions between those working on conflict and on fragility, as those concepts may be overlapping but not identical.[25] In order to address these tensions, DFID's Conflict, Humanitarian and Security Department (CHASE) is completing a Conflict Policy, designed to mainstream conflict prevention throughout the department.[26]

Of the three main UK departments, the FCO is less persuaded of the value of a whole of government approach, because it lacks an operational culture and fears encroachments on its traditional leadership in foreign affairs. It is even less convinced of the utility of working through a "fragile states" lens. It is skittish about labeling countries in its diplomatic work as "fragile"; indeed, most desk officers engage in significant pushback at the idea of classifying their countries of focus as fragile, even for internal studies. More broadly, the FCO has an at-times strained relationship with DFID, as the foreign ministry is still adapting to the loss of foreign aid resources—and direction over development policy—with the creation of an independent development ministry in 1997.

Within the FCO the focal point for work on weak and failing states is the Conflict Issues Group (CIG), established in 2004 to bring together expertise and resources related to conflict and to mainstream conflict analyses, functions previously scattered through the department. The CIG manages the FCO's involvement with the two conflict pools, as well as other FCO programs with their own funds relating to conflict, serving as a liaison with DFID and the MoD on conflict issues, and as the main FCO point of contact with the PCRU. The CIG now has four teams working on peacekeeping and peacebuilding (including UN Security Council resolutions); police and transitional justice; secondments of civilians for deployment to the field; and conflict prevention (to provide oversight of FCO involvement into CRI analyses).[27]

For its part, the MoD welcomes integration of departmental efforts on fragile states as a means to enlist civilian capabilities in stabilizing post-conflict and conflict-prone countries, freeing up the military to conduct its core mission of war-fighting, and offering an "exit strategy" from postwar settings. The MoD is particularly supportive of the Africa Conflict Prevention Pool, because these funds cover nearly all of its work on the continent (beyond bilateral defense relations and arms trade). At the same time, the MoD is frequently frustrated by what it perceives as the lack of a coherent UK vision of national security priorities—or even a document similar to the US *National Security Strategy*—and worries that UK military assets may increasingly be diverted to secondary activities.

Interdepartmental Coordination

Cross-Whitehall decision making appears to be less afflicted with the sort of interagency warfare common within the US system. While rivalries and resistance to whole of government approaches occasionally surface at lower levels, collaboration at senior levels tends to be collegial and constructive, based on the realization that success cannot be delivered through one department alone. At the same time, the decentralized structure of the UK government, which gives cabinet departments immense autonomy, creates disincentives to cross-Whitehall harmonization of policy. Even where common strategic frameworks exist, effective collaboration remains highly dependent on informal networks of individuals and the contingent alignment of personal, political, and departmental incentives.

A major structural impediment to joined-up approaches is the lack of a strong, central coordinating entity with directive authority over the individual departments. The Cabinet Office, despite its placement at the heart of government, is generally incapable of pushing departments toward the pursuit of common strategic goals. Although it ensures that departments follow up on prime ministerial decisions, it otherwise adopts a "light touch," rarely seeking to impose its views but instead serving as the guardian of the principle of cabinet government, providing a neutral setting where the wishes of all ministers may be accurately reflected and represented, and where ministers can engage in the pragmatic search for a solution and build consensus behind a common approach.[28] Moreover, the Cabinet Office has a small staff and little analytic capability to generate strategies on its own. Within the UK government, however, no other office has the authority to ensure coherence and coordination across agencies.

Integrated Country Assessments, Strategic Plans, and Early Warning Systems

The UK government does not yet have an institutionalized process for assessing fragility in developing countries, drafting government-wide strategic country plans setting out how the UK should respond, or determining how foreign assistance and other instruments should be deployed to support these strategies. In current practice, UK embassies generate country plans based on broad principles set by the UK government, but these are not tied closely to strategic goals, nor do they reflect an interdepartmental, whole of government approach.

The main effort to institutionalize a cross-Whitehall strategy for weak and failing states has been the Countries at Risk of Instability (CRI) initiative spearheaded by the Prime Minister's Strategy Unit (PMSU). As outlined in the 2004 report *Investing in Prevention*, the CRI methodology envisions the Cabinet Office secretariat convening cross-Whitehall teams to formulate a common UK strategy for countries in crisis. The CRI team would forge common understanding of the strands of UK involvement in each country; the risks and drivers of instability there; the impact of failure on various UK interests; the priority objectives for UK policy; the tools and instruments at the UK's disposal; and the range of options (with associated costs) available to policymakers.

Among other benefits, the CRI process is intended to encourage the buy-in of each department by highlighting the implications of instability for its own interests, for instance by threatening the achievement of the Millennium Development

Goals (DFID), undermining regional stability (FCO), endangering energy security (Department for International Trade), providing a safe haven for terrorists (MoD), or threatening uncontrolled immigration or facilitating organized crime (Home Office). Although there will be inevitable tensions and trade-offs in departmental objectives and UK priorities, as well as debates over what tools to use, the key is to look for "win-win" interventions. Ultimately, the ensuing strategy would be related to high-level UK strategic goals.

To date, the government has conducted CRI assessments on several countries deemed at risk of instability, including Bangladesh, Nigeria, Burma, and Jamaica. In each case, there has been an effort to identify key UK interests, such as in the areas of trade, immigration, drugs, WMD, Islamic fundamentalism, and energy security, etc. These CRI assessments have included discussions not only across government in London but with missions, multinational companies, NGOs, diaspora groups, and academics.

The PMSU assumed that the Cabinet Office itself would create a small interdepartmental team to undertake joint strategic analyses of target countries, using CRI's sophisticated methodology for assessing risks of instability. Instead, the Cabinet Office decided to rely on existing departmental capacities, choosing different lead agencies depending on the country of focus. This has essentially ensured bureaucratic resistance and forced the UK to reinvent the wheel on each occasion. As a result, there is still no robust joint analytical capability within the managerial level at the core of Whitehall. Instead, the Cabinet Office, on an ad hoc basis and as requested by the Prime Minister's Foreign Policy Strategy Group, manages the interdepartmental generation of assessments of particular countries of interest.

Furthermore, despite mapping out a process, the CRI has not had much traction across Whitehall, as powerful ministers remain reluctant to concede to coordination from the center or to give up control over spending decisions. In each case, it has been a struggle to gain departmental buy-in, with the MoD and particularly the FCO resisting to cede autonomy, and claiming that they already conduct their own analyses.[29] In reality, such stove-piped analyses by single departments tend to miss the cross-sector linkages that contribute to the dynamics of instability and failure.[30] In the few cases where the CRI process has been tried, it has led to some refocusing of resources and attention. But it is too early to say that it will stimulate truly comprehensive strategies, backed by dedicated resources.

In addition, the UK remains internally divided over the proper nature and role of early warning, with particular differences over time horizons. For the MoD, early warning might mean within six months; for the FCO, slightly longer; and for DFID, several years. The FCO is exploring statistical models of indicators for early warning, but there is no process to generate a list of, say, twenty-five countries at risk of instability. The Cabinet Office has its own assessment staff, the Joint Intelligence Committee (JIC), which is responsible for drafting consensus assessments of the UK intelligence community on pressing matters, including providing periodic "traffic light" watch lists of countries for various purposes.

Nor is there any regular means for moving from early warning to early action. The UK government does not have sufficient systems in place to come up with a country strategy, or to determine where money should go if early warning and analysis suggests there is a problem. Ideally, one would want an agreed methodology for indicators of instability or fragility, and a mechanism to bring crisis countries to the attention of the Foreign Policy Strategy Group. But any response would have resource implications, forcing the Cabinet Office to go cap in hand to the departments, none of which wants to bear this burden. One way to get around this problem would be for funds to be held centrally, within the Cabinet Office, so that the line ministries could be forced to realign their proposals and policies to gain access to these resources. The problem currently is that when a crisis strikes, all agency budgets are already programmed. As a result, agencies tend to treat the conflict pools as a contingency fund, with the risk that the pools will be raided to address short-term crises rather than long-term conflict prevention.

One assumption behind CRI, borne out by experience, is that it is essential to try to achieve "jointness" as far upstream as possible, through common analysis of the problem. Besides resulting in a more accurate understanding of the dynamics of instability, the process of joint assessment itself can break down cultural and institutional barriers to collaboration. A caveat to this observation is that there should be interdepartmental clarity about what one is assessing (for example, fragility, risk of conflict, or danger to UK national interests). Indeed, one problematic trend within the UK government has been the promotion of competing assessment frameworks and methodologies, including so-called "drivers of change analyses" (DFID), joint stability assessments (PCRU), and instability assessments (CRI).

There are other lessons of the CRI experience for whole of government approaches. First, a high-level remit from the government is essential to generate momentum for interdepartmental collaboration. In the case of CRI, the imprimatur of the prime minister himself was important for getting cabinet departments to at least take the effort seriously. Second, cultivating stakeholder buy-in is essential. The PMSU was not as sensitive as it might have been to bureaucratic concerns, and its grand ambitions threatened and alienated some potential allies; arguably, a more incremental approach might have paid bigger dividends. Third, political will for integrated approaches can be generated if policymakers are given concrete options with associated cost implications. Finally, the mainstreaming of joined-up government approaches must be institutionalized as a quasi-automatic process, or else it will remain periodic and ad hoc.

Funding Instruments: The Conflict Pools

The UK's most innovative instruments to promote whole of government engagement in fragile states are the Africa Conflict Prevention Pool and the Global Conflict Prevention Pool, created in 2001 among DFID, the MoD, and the FCO to develop a common strategic approach to resolving conflicts and rationalizing the allocation of financial resources in this effort.[31] The integration of these various departments underscores that the failed state challenge is at once a security, foreign policy, and developmental challenge. The pools have enjoyed success, by encouraging more coherent analysis across departments, particularly with respect to Africa; reducing time lags for the provision of urgent needs; and facilitating the development of joint country and sub-regional strategies informed by conflict assessments. Each pool is supervised by a committee of ministers and is governed by a Public Service Agreement (PSA) monitored by the Treasury Department, and agreements have been reached on standards for accessing pool resources.

When the pools were first created, each department put money in a pot, from which the three departments could draw for common initiatives. (Today, the pools represent additional resources, not from ministerial budgets.) Unsurprisingly, the pools started with a number of legacy activities, with an effort to justify these on whole of government grounds. Over time, there has been an effort to force the departments to try to develop genuinely tripartite strategies that are more honed and targeted. There is some evidence of a socialization process, with increased dialogue and coherence. At the same time, the transaction costs associated with developing common strategies have been significant.

For both pools, strategies are chosen out of a competitive bidding process. Potential bids are developed within a tri-departmental process and then sent to a tri-departmental steering group, which passes its recommendations and options on to the cabinet ministers for approval. The main criteria for funding are whether the conflict is important to the UK government; whether assistance from the UK can make a difference on the ground; whether a joint interdepartmental effort will have powerful synergies; and whether the UK can hope to leverage other donors in the effort. In considering whether to approve proposed strategies, departments are asked to prioritize their baseline objectives and to state the minimum amount they need to make a difference.

The Africa Conflict Prevention Pool (ACPP)

Following a review in 2000, the UK cabinet decided to establish a common pool for Africa.[32] Capitalized at £63 million, the ACPP is managed by DFID. It focuses on building African capacity in conflict management, advancing conflict prevention and post-conflict reconstruction in different sub-regional priority areas and conflicts, supporting pan-African initiatives for security sector reform, and addressing the economic causes of conflicts. Initially, the Africa Pool was reactive, dominated by efforts to secure and consolidate peace deals in West and Central Africa, particularly in Sierra Leone (which remains the biggest single recipient, taking some 25 percent of the pool's resources). It has since become more forward looking, seeking to bolster the emerging African Peace and Security Architecture, including improving the AU's capacity for early warning and the African Standby Force. The current top priorities for the ACPP (as defined by the tripartite PSA to Reduce Conflict in Africa) are Sierra Leone, Nigeria, Sudan, and the Democratic Republic of Congo (DRC). The general consensus within the UK government is that the pool remains a "work in progress" but is "doing some good."[33]

Like the Global Pool, the Africa Pool is allocated on a bidding basis.[34] Proposals are meant to fit into one of five overarching strategies. One is a pan-African strategy reflecting commitments made by the UK at the G-8 and other forums. The other four are regional strategies for West Africa, the Horn and East Africa, the Great Lakes, and Southern Africa. These regional strategies provide a framework for interdepartmental teams at UK embassies to bid.[35] Officials in London screen the proposals, horse-trade among themselves, and advise an interagency board of directors, who then make recommendations to the Cabinet. Once the Cabinet approves the strategies, the money goes back to agencies for actual expenditure and implementation. Many strategies are rolled over from the previous year. The MoD currently spends about half of the Pool's resources, in large part because military operations tend to be more expensive than civilian ones.

Global Conflict Prevention Pool (GCPP)

The GCPP,[36] managed by the FCO, had a budget of £74 million in 2006, slightly larger than the ACPP. It currently funds fifteen distinct strategies, including twelve country or regional and three thematic strategies. Despite the "prevention" label, in most cases the strategies are devoted to countries that are in—or emerging from—conflict. The allocations for 2006 include £12.5 million for Iraq and £20 million for Afghanistan (split evenly between a main country strategy and a counternarcotics strategy). If one adds in the £8 million for the Balkans, approximately half of the GCPP is allocated to these three contingencies. The remaining twelve strategies (including one for India-Pakistan) are as small as £1 million, and more than half are £2 million or less. In interviews with the authors of this study, several UK officials wondered what impact strategies could really have on conflict prevention at such modest levels of funding. The Global Pool has limited flexibility, moreover, because only one strategy to date has been terminated, whereas several others have been added, diluting what can be spent. Likewise, there is broad sentiment that the intensity of UK involvement in Iraq and Afghanistan merits funding out of other pots, and leaving the pools for areas of narrower UK involvement that might not otherwise secure resources.

How Do The Pools Stack Up?

The two pools have improved the coherence of UK policy toward weak and failing states, particularly by encouraging dialogue, information sharing and—to some degree—harmonization of departmental approaches in crisis countries. The process of devising common strategies helps ensure that inevitable tensions in departmental priorities and approaches will be exposed, rather than remaining buried or obscured, forcing stakeholders to fight and sort it out in vigorous debates over what the pools are for and what constitutes a legitimate pool activity.

Of the two pools, the Africa Pool is widely considered to be more coherent and focused than the Global Pool, which tends to be more subject to political pressures and raiding from departments. Interviewees attributed the ACPP's success to several factors. First, it was built by organizing existing units across departments rather than being created out of whole cloth, which has helped to promote buy-in and ownership from the relevant departments. Second, the pool is coordinated by DFID, which has a longer time horizon than the FCO (which manages the Global Pool) and is better at putting assistance packages together, delivering services, bolstering institutions, and tracking outcomes. Third, the Africa Pool has a lower profile than the Global Pool, which is more subject to pressure for quick results, allowing the ACPP to work within a medium-term framework and with more realistic expectations and better pacing of interventions. Finally, the ACPP has been aided by the perceived seriousness of African governments in creating the AU and the New Partnership for Africa's Development (NEPAD).

Observers frequently invoke the UK's Conflict Pools as innovative instruments worthy of emulation by the donor community. The reality is more nuanced. Although they are certainly "better than nothing," in the words of several UK officials, they are also "dysfunctional" in important respects, and have not delivered genuine cross-Whitehall strategies. To begin with, the pools face a recurrent danger of being raided by departments, particularly the FCO and the MoD, which seek flexible, unallocated funds to finance pressing contingencies. The UK government faces a constant balancing act between insulating these modest resources for conflict prevention purposes and drawing on them for urgent needs.

Second, instead of being used strategically, to ensure a unified approach tailored to a given environment, the pools are often treated as licenses for individual departments to do what they already intended to do, using their own tools, without thinking about how these might be integrated. That is, the pools do not always provide an incentive to cooperate on a common strategy, so much as a tempting basket of resources to exploit for departmental aims. The pools would be more functional if they were placed under control of the Cabinet Office, with the power to impose discipline, but the latter has not accepted this role.

In addition, there is no authoritative mechanism to evaluate and adjudicate among the various objectives that the UK government ought to be pursuing in focus countries, or agree on the various tools that it should bring to bear in attaining these ends. The various players tend to have different strategic priorities: whereas both the MoD and DFID recognize that security and development are mutually reinforcing, the former is focused first and foremost on *security* outcomes, the latter on *development* outcomes. It remains ambiguous as to whether the ACPP and GCPP funds should be driven primarily by UK national security and national interest considerations, or by the more disinterested goals of poverty alleviation, conflict prevention, and human security. On the one hand, the Public Service Agreements governing the use of the pools do not use the phrase "national interests." On the other hand, at least half of the funds in the Global Pool are devoted to countries or regions—Afghanistan, Iraq, and the Balkans—where the UK's national interests are strongly and directly engaged. Particularly in "hot" conflicts, such as Afghanistan, there are frequent frictions over how to link short- and long-term priorities for the use of pool funds.

The main lesson of the pools is that common resources do not necessarily create common understandings and harmonized objectives. As one UK official notes, "Joining up money does not ensure joined up strategy."[37] Resources must respond to the defini-tion of the problem and the formulation of strategy—and not the other way around. Even when pools promote joint thinking, they may not promote joint programming and implementation. In many cases, UK teams have cobbled departmental concerns into a "common strategy," only to go their own way once the money has been doled out in addressing their specific component. To discourage departments from using the pools as slush funds to do what they would have done in any event, the steering groups have begun requiring annual reporting on how "jointness" is occurring in the field.[38]

Finally, even when they work as advertised, the pools remain extremely modest compared with the challenge posed by fragile states. They cannot be expected to have a significant impact compared to other programs managed by the government. Subjects interviewed also noted the difficulty of finding metrics to assess the relative contribution of the modest pool resources, compared with many other contextual factors, in helping to mitigate conflict.

The UK's Comprehensive Spending Review is expected to renew and perhaps even expand the conflict pools. There may be a move to rebalance the current portfolio, currently split between many smaller strategies and several larger ones. There is also a possibility that the two pools will be consolidated—a step that could be warranted, provided that the unified pool is not simply treated as a target to be raided (resulting in a diminution of aid allocated to Africa). Finally, there is an outside chance that the pools could be replaced by a more comprehensive funding instrument that seeks not only to tackle conflict but a broader array of perceived transnational threats, including crime and terrorism. While superficially appealing, such a move could also be unwieldy, leading to greater political infighting for resources to engage in activities already programmed.

Outside the Pools: Pilot Project—Yemen

Beyond the pools themselves, the UK has developed whole of government pilot strategies in several countries. One of the most notable is an ongoing initiative in Yemen, undertaken by the FCO, DFID, MoD, and the UK intelligence services. This effort, coordinated by the Cabinet Office and funded by DFID, has included a common assessment of the problems facing that country, the UK's interests there, the resources and tools at the UK's disposal, and the desirable strategy for deploying and sequencing these. The effort originated with a "Drivers of Change" study in September 2004, designed to improve the UK's understanding of the political, social, economic and environmental conditions in Yemen. In response to a request from the UK embassy in Sana'a in early 2005 for a more coherent policy, the prime minister's office instructed the Cabinet Office to work with the FCO and other departments on a comprehensive whole of government approach to Yemen. The resulting strategy emerged in mid-2005.

Several factors facilitated cross-Whitehall adoption of an integrated approach to Yemen. First and most importantly, the initiative enjoyed high-level buy-in, including from the Prime Minister's Office itself, as well as official sanction from the government in Sana'a. Second, the country "ticked the relevant boxes" for each department, since it had implications for regional stability, poverty alleviation, counter-terrorism, and intelligence. Third, Yemen was a small country of modest importance to the UK government (though with a history of British involvement) and with a relatively small number of UK actors on the ground. In contrast with a high-profile case like Iraq or Afghanistan, it was unlikely to become a source of political infighting and turf wars. (The paradoxical lesson would appear to be that where the stakes are lower, the prospects for collaboration are higher). Fourth, the interagency assessment and planning process was drawn out over a period of nine months, permitting sufficient time to build up a common understanding among departments of the challenges confronting Yemen and what needed to be done. Fifth, despite differences in their priority goals, the relevant UK departments came to understand that they needed to do things in different ways. The FCO, for its part, came to recognize that development was a key element to the realization of UK foreign policy objectives in Yemen. DFID, similarly, recognized that progress on human development required more thoroughgoing changes in the country's governance.

Because the program is still in its infancy, it is too early to make a definitive assessment of its impact. Nevertheless, several tentative conclusions can be drawn. On the positive side, the joined-up approach has fostered a common understanding in the UK of local conditions, as well as socializing the FCO and the MoD to see development as critical to achieving HMG's foreign policy and national security goals in the country. In the words of one analyst, "DFID has been able to make the case—by and large accepted by its government counterparts—that security and stability in Yemen (and regionally) cannot be assured if underlying problems relating to poverty, poor governance, and conflict are not addressed."[39]

More negatively, the interagency strategic framework developed for Yemen is better at diagnosing the current situation than at prescribing specific actions each UK department should take to advance development, democratic government, and security in the country. It provides less of an action plan, moreover, than a description of what UK agencies are already doing in these key areas. The main exception is the Integrated Justice Sector Development (IJSD) initiative, the only significant instance of joint UK programming. Led and financed by DFID, with the involvement of the FCO, the MoD, and the PCRU (Post-Conflict Reconstruction Unit), the IJSD is intended to provide a comprehensive approach to addressing policing and justice issues. Because these arenas transcend traditional departmental boundaries, the design and implementation of programs require continual communication and harmonization both among UK government departments and their counterpart ministries in the Yemeni government.

One of the main lessons of the Yemen experience is that the UK needs more foreign assistance that can be made available for non-traditional development activities in fragile states. Although DFID has entered the security domain through its work on police and justice issues, it is constrained from addressing other critical SSR activities, such as reform of the armed forces and intelligence services. The FCO and MoD, which are intensely interested in addressing these needs, lack funds of their own to do so. This suggests that HMG should consider creating additional funding instruments to address SSR challenges "which are on the margins of ODA-ability."[40]

Post-Conflict Reconstruction Unit

In addition to the Conflict Prevention Pools, the most notable institutional innovation to address the problem of fragile states in an integrated fashion is the Post-Conflict Reconstruction Unit (PCRU), created in summer 2004 to provide the UK with a more robust civilian capability to deploy alongside military forces in the aftermath of violent conflict, and to inject greater strategic coherence into UK post-conflict operations. The PCRU has a cap of thirty-four permanent slots (twenty-eight currently filled), drawn from all three departments. It responds to a four-person board of directors composed of its main stakeholders (MoD, DFID, FCO, and Cabinet Office), which in turn reports to the Conflict Prevention and Reconstruction Committee in Cabinet (which also governs the pools). DFID supplies the PCRU with its modest operating budget, limited to £10 million, including £4 million for running the office and £6 million for equipment costs, logistics, and deployment of staff to the field. The PCRU has no large source of program funds.

The initial expectation was that the PCRU would lead UK engagement in crisis countries, including not only defining the strategy but also running the operations. Despite early ambitions, the PCRU was created with an ambiguous mandate and quickly became the object of interdepartmental infighting and turf battles. The main UK departments rebuffed the PCRU's aspirations for a directive and operational role, arguing that in most crisis situations, the UK government would have adequate mechanisms at headquarters and many of the relevant pieces on the ground. Although there was a vigorous discussion about giving the PCRU the lead in the UK's involvement in Helmand Province in Afghanistan, for example, departments resisted this move strongly. Lacking either the political leverage of the departments or demonstrated assets or capabilities to take on this project, the PCRU found it difficult to argue against this decision. The PCRU thus found its mandate downsized, primarily as a locus of strategic planning and capacity building in support of other government departments.

The PCRU currently has five distinct functions. The first is to develop a *stability assessment framework* that can be employed when Cabinet determines that a crisis critical to UK interests merits the insertion of UK troops. More action oriented than either the CRI assessments or DFID's "conflict assessment framework," this is intended to permit UK officials to analyze what needs to be done to bring stability on the ground in the short and medium term. Second, the PCRU is working with the MoD's Development, Concepts and Doctrine Center to develop a *joint civil-military doctrine* that will bring civilian departments, particularly the FCO and DFID, into comprehensive campaign planning for UK military interventions and post-conflict reconstruction and stabilization efforts.[41] (This planning tool has been employed to help shape the UK's involvement in Helmand.) Third, to implement these reconstruction plans, the PCRU is helping to create a *deployable civilian capability*, composed of core staff from the PCRU itself, consultants, and longer-term contractors. Fourth, the office is engaged in *capacity building for regional and sub-regional organizations*, particularly in Africa. Finally, the office is feeding *lessons learned* into future operations, by the distillation and integration of best practices into national and multinational exercises and evolving doctrine.

The PCRU's lack of clout reflects several factors. One is its awkward bureaucratic position. Under the original conception, the Cabinet Office would have hosted the PCRU, which would have underlined its centrality at the core of Whitehall. Unfortunately, Cabinet declined to take on such an operational responsibility. Accordingly, the PCRU was established as a free-floating entity, lacking either a natural departmental power base or clear authority from the center.

Another dilemma is that the PCRU was created in response to Afghanistan and Iraq, which many now regard as anomalous, since the appetite for such large-scale ventures is close to nil across the UK political spectrum. Moreover, the PCRU's practical role in both of these countries has been very modest.[42] In the absence of a clear mission on the horizon, the PCRU thus faces something of an existential crisis, forced to persuade other departments of its continued relevance, and placed in the uncomfortable position of touting for business. This raises the question of how specialized agencies like the PCRU can be empowered, and how they can gain credibility, without actually being given something to run. (As one interviewee noted, until it gets its "hands dirty" with a real mission, there will be doubts about its value added.) One unanswered question is whether the PCRU will act in contingencies, such as UN missions, when the UK lacks a military presence of its own. Although DFID is keen on this possibility, the MOD worries about detracting from the PCRU's core business, and creating pressure for deployment of UK troops in secondary theaters.

In the words of one interviewee, the PCRU "typifies the problem of creating a whole of government unit in a hurry, in a complex issue area, without prior consensus among stakeholders on the strategy and what you want to achieve." Indeed, the unit was created prior to broad agreement about its objectives, mandates, capabilities, and authorities.[43] One of the lessons is that it is unrealistic to presume an institutional fix will overcome the political failure to resolve fundamental differences of outlook and objectives, or turf wars within government.

Conclusion

While the UK's whole of government approach to fragile states is head and shoulders above those of most other donors working in this area, it remains very much a work in progress. Its future policies and instruments are now in flux, as the government undergoes its zero-based Comprehensive Spending Review (CSR), which will force departments to justify to the Treasury Department everything that they are now doing. One area of special concern for the Treasury is whether HMG is currently spending enough on the theme of "global instability." Many topics will be up for grabs, among them the relationship between early warning and response; the future of the Conflict Pools; the desirable scope and role of the PCRU; and the role of the Foreign Policy Strategy Group. The CSR may well result in a reallocation of current resources toward fragile states. As part of the CSR, DFID has proposed a tripartite review, to be undertaken with the FCO and the MoD, to examine what HMG is doing in the areas of conflict and security. In principle, this could go well beyond the pools themselves, to instill even more joined-up approaches in designing country strategies and funding mechanisms across the departments.

Chapter Two

The United States

Overview

Despite the growing prominence of "weak and failing states" in US foreign policy discourse, the United States lags behind Great Britain in developing an integrated, whole of government strategy to respond to the challenges and dilemmas posed by fragile states. In the wake of Afghanistan and Iraq, the US government has taken initial steps to build a standing interagency capability for stabilization and reconstruction. It has been far more tentative in developing a government-wide strategy—with aligned objectives, motivations, resources, and activities—to help ameliorate underlying causes of fragility, instability, and conflict in the developing world. Among US government departments and agencies, only the United States Agency for International Development (USAID) has adopted an explicit fragile states strategy. There is little movement to adopt a more integrated, government-wide approach that could bring all relevant instruments of national power and influence to bear in reforming or bolstering institutions in some of the world's most precarious countries. The reform of US foreign assistance announced in January 2006 could in principle foster greater coherence in US policy by encouraging more effective alignment of aid and policy. But the current design suffers from a relative inattention to the specific problem of state fragility, and from practical constraints on the power of the new Director of Foreign Assistance.

Several aspects of the current US approach are distinctive and noteworthy. First and most profoundly, US engagement with weak and failing states is motivated almost entirely by national security concerns. Indeed, to the degree that the Bush administration seeks an integrated, whole of government approach toward fragile states, its overriding priority is less to advance "policy coherence for development" than to ensure "policy coherence for national security." Second, the United States to date has invested far more energy and resources in developing doctrine and capabilities to conduct post-conflict operations than in helping prevent state collapse to begin with, through measures of poverty alleviation and institution-building. Third, compared to its international partners, the United States relies more heavily on military than civilian instruments in engaging with conflict prone and war-torn countries. While it has taken initial steps to develop civilian capabilities to share this burden, these initiatives continue to lack adequate political support from the Bush administration, and funding from Congress. Fourth, the US approach to fragile and war-torn states elevates democracy as the ultimate goal of US engagement, based on the assumption that democratization and state-building efforts necessarily go hand in hand, whereas other donors have focused on the less ambitious—though still challenging—goals of effective institutions and "good enough governance." Finally, the United States under the Bush administration has pursued a distinctively unilateral posture in the pursuit of national security, foreign, and development policy, and its approach toward weak, fragile, and post-conflict states is no exception. American policy places little emphasis on the need to harmonize US approaches with those of other donors, or indeed to align these policies with the priorities of local actors.

A New Focus on Weak, Failing, and Post-Conflict States

The driving forces behind increased US interest in weak and failing states are unquestionably the terrorist attacks of September 11, 2001, and the subsequent difficulties the United States encountered in stabilizing Afghanistan and Iraq following US-led invasions of those countries. Prior to 9/11, most US policymakers (irrespective of political allegiances) viewed fragile states primarily through a humanitarian lens, as being potential sites of violent conflict, atrocities, and human suffering. During the 1990s, Democrats were more likely than Republicans to support armed intervention for humanitarian protection purposes, and the increasingly multidimensional nature of UN peace operations. Yet, with few exceptions (in the Balkans, or Haiti, for example), the US policy community was united in according such countries marginal geopolitical importance. Such states were, at best, remote and third-tier security concerns.

The attacks on the World Trade Center and the Pentagon changed this calculus, showing that transnational threats could in fact emanate from some of the world's poorest and most dysfunctional countries. Al Qaeda's ability to inflict enormous damage on the United States from a base in Afghanistan persuaded President Bush and his advisors, in the words of the 2002 National Security Strategy, that America "is now more threatened by weak and failing states than we are by conquering ones."[44] This new view quickly became conventional wisdom within US foreign policy and national security circles, and weak states were increasingly associated with real or perceived transnational threats, including drug trafficking, terrorism, and organized crime that could have serious consequences for the United States. In an age of global threats, national security was increasingly tied to internal conditions within other states. Such thinking percolated throughout the US government. In 2003, USAID issued a White Paper that drew attention to the global threats posed by weak states: "terrorism, political violence, civil wars, organized crime, drug trafficking, infectious diseases, environmental crises, refugee flows and mass migration cascade across the borders of weak states more destructively than ever before."[45] This thinking was rearticulated in USAID's Fragile States Strategy of 2005[46], as well as the National Security Strategy of 2006, which placed an increased emphasis on the importance of democracy promotion as a way of building effective and well-functioning states.[47] One consequence of this strategic reorientation was to elevate development to the position of a third "pillar" of US national security policy, along with defense and diplomacy.

Simultaneously, the Department of Defense has expanded its focus of operations to weak and unstable states in the developing world. The most recent National Defense Strategy and the Quadrennial Defense Review depart from a traditional focus on interstate war by, among other things, calling on the US military to strengthen the sovereign capacities of friendly governments to control their territories against internal threats of terrorism, insurgency, and crime. Beyond expanded training of foreign security forces, the Pentagon has pushed a comprehensive US strategy to address the world's "ungoverned areas," where states lack the capacity or will to control their territory against those that may wish to do harm to the US and its allies.[48] The Central Intelligence Agency—which has identified fifty such zones globally—is said to be devoting new collection assets to long-neglected parts of the world.[49] The National Intelligence Council (NIC) has launched a political instability watch list to identify states at risk of collapse, so that the US government can launch conflict prevention and mitigation efforts.[50]

This new policy attention to weak and failed states has been reinforced by evident shortcomings of the United States and its international partners in stabilizing and reconstructing post-invasion Afghanistan and Iraq. These failures stimulated an effort to improve US capabilities to rebuild war-torn societies. In 2004, the State Department responded by creating an office to lead interagency efforts to plan, prepare, and implement such operations. In parallel, the Department of Defense has approved a directive embracing stabilization operations as a "core mission" of the US military. Likewise, USAID has created an Office of Military Affairs to improve coherence and coordination with the US military on development-related issues.

Finally, the State Department's "transformational diplomacy" initiative, announced in January 2006, and the subsequent foreign aid reforms, are motivated in large part by the fear that weak and failing states in the developing world, if left alone, may become conveyor belts of "global bads" for the US and its allies. As Secretary of State Condoleezza Rice has explained, the goal of these reforms is to "build and sustain democratic, well-governed states that will respond to the needs of their people and conduct themselves responsibly in the international system."[51] For the State Department, this means, among other things, redeploying diplomats to global hot spots. For foreign aid, it implies injecting greater strategic coherence and coordination into the woefully fragmented assistance regime, which has aid trickling out of twenty-odd spigots across the US government, addressing everything from health interventions to democracy promotion to law enforcement cooperation.

A Common Strategic Vision?

In sum, five years after 9/11, this new strategic orientation has informed a flurry of development, defense, intelligence, and diplomatic initiatives. Across US agencies, multiple strategies, white papers, and other guiding policy documents have been and are being developed to respond to the US preoccupation with weak, failing, and post-conflict states. Despite this superficial unanimity, the US response to fragile states remains fragmented, and to some degree inconsistent. While there is broad rhetorical agreement that the problems of poor governance, instability, and war-torn states require integrated, "3D" approaches (through merging defense, diplomacy, and development) the US government has yet to forge interagency consensus on the rationale for US engagement; the criteria that should guide US involvement; the scale of US aspirations; the end state toward which these efforts should be directed; and the means required to achieve success. In post-conflict settings, for example, should the goal be the restoration of baseline order, the creation of a functioning government, or a liberal democracy? This is not an abstract question. A constant challenge in engaging fragile states will be to negotiate the tensions and trade-offs between short-term expediency driven by political and security concerns, and the long-term imperatives of institution building, which should be informed by development considerations.

The US approach is rather a messy amalgam of the dominant preoccupations of the Department of Defense, State Department, and USAID, oftentimes in that order. Broadly speaking, the

Pentagon views fragile and post-conflict states primarily through a national security prism, as part of a larger counterterrorist and counterinsurgency agenda, with a particular focus on the Muslim world; the State Department is preoccupied with transforming a wider range of weak and war-torn states into effective democracies; and USAID regards state weakness as a developmental challenge to be addressed by working with local actors to create the institutional foundations of good governance and economic growth. The United States has come a long way in a short period of time, but the multiple initiatives and approaches being adopted do not yet constitute a clear vision, much less a unified strategy.

Perhaps surprisingly, given its modest bureaucratic clout, USAID has been ahead of the other US agencies in identifying fragile states firmly as a core component of its work and in integrating conflict prevention and mitigation into its activities. In 2002, Administrator Andrew Natsios created a USAID office of Conflict Management and Mitigation, in the hopes of mainstreaming sensitivity to conflict dynamics into everything that USAID does in developing countries. Subsequently, USAID's White Paper of 2004 placed fragile states firmly among the five criteria for providing development assistance, which should be designed to support "stabilization, security, reform and capacity development in countries characterized by instability and weak governance."[52]

More recently, the 2005 USAID *Fragile States Strategy* underlined the special circumstances and development challenges of weak and failing states. The paper classifies fragile states into two general categories: *vulnerable* states—those unwilling or unable to provide security and basic services to their people, and where the legitimacy of the government may be in question—and *crisis* states, which are at great risk of violent conflict. Broadly speaking, the goal of US policy should be "reversing decline in fragile states and advancing their recovery to a stage where transformational development is possible," including by enhancing stability through the cessation of conflict; fostering an improvement in the security situation; encouraging policy reform, including through engagement with civil society; and helping to develop institutional capacity. In its programming, USAID advocates engaging strategically and selectively; focusing on the sources of state fragility; linking short-term impact with long-term structural reform; and setting appropriate goals and targets that reflect realities within the country itself. To help mainstream the concept of fragility within USAID, and monitor global trends, the agency has created a Fragile States Council.

Despite these conceptual and institutional innovations, USAID has had little success in winning broader interagency buy-in for the concept of state "fragility." Indeed, the concept has become almost entirely marginalized since early 2006, when the administration announced a sweeping foreign assistance reform (discussed below). These reforms have pulled USAID further under the State Department, with both positive and negative ramifications. On the one hand, it promises to bring senior USAID leadership into the corridors of power at the State Department. On the other hand, it is likely to threaten what is left of USAID's independence, subordinating the aid agency's historic mandate of promoting poverty alleviation and economic growth to short-term projects more aligned with current national security preoccupations, including fighting the war against terrorism, and democracy promotion.

Post-Conflict Reconstruction and Stabilization

To date, the United States has devoted far more attention and resources to improving US performance in post-conflict operations than to preventing state collapse in the first place. The primary institutional innovations have been the creation of a new State Department office intended to coordinate reconstruction and stabilization efforts across the US government, and a belated recognition by the Department of Defense that stability operations are today a core mission of the US military. The overriding impetus for these changes was the debacle of inadequate postwar planning for Iraq and the subsequent U.S. failure to advance peace, political stability and economic revival in that country.

A New State Department Office

Under President Clinton, the National Security Council had developed a sophisticated political-military planning process, formalized in Presidential Decision Directive 56, outlining the roles and responsibilities of US agencies in "complex contingency operations."[53] Upon taking office, President George W. Bush abandoned the directive. As a result, the United States went to war in Iraq without having a comprehensive plan for "winning the peace." Both USAID and the State Department were culpable in this outcome, for it was the very lack of standing civilian operational capabilities that encouraged the White House to transfer all responsibility for the post-conflict phase to the Department of Defense. The chaos that ensued after the invasion—including the breakdown of law and order, the collapse of public services, and the onset of a full-fledged insurgency—drove home the price of failing to develop the doctrine and capabilities needed to stabilize and reconstruct war-torn societies and led to Congressional agitation for improving the capacity of the United States to respond to these contingencies.

By spring of 2004, a consensus transcending partisan divides had taken hold: in a world of failed states and terrorist threats, reconstruction and stabilization were no longer sidelines of US global engagement, but were core missions of foreign and national security policy. To meet this challenge, the United States needed a robust standing capacity, including both civilian and military components, to conduct and manage post-conflict operations. Essential ingredients of this approach would include new coordination mechanisms with clear lines of authority and accountability; a robust process for contingency planning; and a deployable civilian capability to permit rapid, effective responses. To fill this gap, the National Security Council in April 2004 agreed that the State Department should coordinate interagency responses to future post-conflict operations, including the development of a civilian surge capacity that could be deployed quickly to crisis countries. To this end, the State Department in August 2004 created an Office of the Coordinator of Reconstruction and Stabilization (S/CRS).

Although the office got to work immediately, its formal interagency authorities were not approved until more than a year after its creation—in December 2005—when the White House released

National Security Presidential Directive (NSPD) 44: "Management of Interagency Efforts Concerning Reconstruction and Stabilization."[54] NSPD 44 assigns to the Secretary of State responsibility to prepare for, plan, coordinate, and implement reconstruction and stabilization operations in a wide range of contingencies, ranging from complex emergencies to failing and failed states, and war-torn societies. The office is, theoretically, supposed to serve as the focal point for creating, managing, and deploying standing civilian response capabilities for a range of purposes, including to advance "internal security, governance and participation, social and economic well-being, and justice and reconciliation."[55] Where the US military may be involved, the office is to coordinate with the Department of Defense to harmonize military and civilian involvement. Significantly, its mandate covers prevention as well as reaction.

While the creation of such an office is a feat unto itself, S/CRS continues to suffer from three fundamental weaknesses that undermine its utility in bringing coherence and clarity to the issue of reconstruction, stabilization, and state fragility across the US government. First, the office was intended to be a focal point for coordination so as to ensure a timely US government response to state failure and reconstruction and stabilization efforts, by reaching back to relevant agencies and developing and drawing upon standing technical capacities to complement the country-specific knowledge that one finds in regional bureaus. But bureaucratic resistance within the State Department itself, intra-agency rivalries and jockeying for power, along with the decision not to have the office take part in the two main US reconstruction efforts of Afghanistan or Iraq, left S/CRS with inadequate authority and respect within the executive branch. As a result, the office—which cannot actually direct agencies—has rarely succeeded in doing any actual coordinating among the different offices. It has been relegated to offering conflict management consultancy services to often skeptical State Department bureaus. Furthermore, it has only established one Country Reconstruction and Stabilization Group, to assist interagency policy coherence in Sudan.

Second, since it was created, S/CRS has been attempting to

fulfill a mandate that is both massive and—in the absence of clear White House support and adequate resources—unrealistic. These aspirations have included creating an early warning system for countries at risk of instability; leading interagency efforts to prevent or mitigate conflict in specific cases; developing joint civil-military doctrine for post-conflict operations; designing and conducting exercises with military counterparts; building standing civilian response capabilities within the State Department, USAID, the wider government and US society; mobilizing and deploying these resources to the field and to the military's Regional Combatant Commands in actual crises; running post-conflict operations in Washington; mainstreaming an appreciation of conflict prevention within the US foreign policy bureaucracy; distilling best practices and lessons learned from post-conflict operations and integrating these into policy; and engaging with international partners.

Third, and related, S/CRS has been chronically underfunded, as the White House and Congress have declined to invest even modest resources in this issue area. For the past two years, the S/CRS office has sought, with lukewarm support from the White House, a modest $100 million Conflict Response Fund to jump-start interagency cooperation for impending post-conflict operations. In both cases, Congress, historically distrustful of "slush funds" not programmed to any specific activity, has rejected the budget item, on the grounds that the administration can simply reprogram existing budgetary allocations, or prepare a supplemental request for unforeseen contingencies, as has been the case for Iraq and Afghanistan.[56] Such a position ignores the time lag required to prepare a supplemental request, and the bureaucratic resistance to reprogramming budget allocations, both of which tend to stymie fast executive branch responses. In reality, there is no substitute for a flexible, rapidly disbursing contingency fund as an incentive to bring parties to the table in days, rather than weeks or months, when an unanticipated crisis emerges. In the absence of adequate contingency funding for civilian operations or joint pooling across departments, the administration has resorted to certain stopgap measures. In the most recent Defense

Authorization Bill, for example, Congress agreed to allow the Secretary of Defense to transfer up to $100 million over two years from the Pentagon to the State Department in the form of goods, services, and funding to support civilian deployment in stability operations.

The office's broad agenda would be unwieldy even under the best of circumstances, implying that S/CRS would not only organize, train, and equip the interagency for stabilization and reconstruction efforts, but also lead planning, deployment, and execution of those operations. It is unreasonable to expect a single understaffed and under-resourced office, operating from one department, to be able to coordinate US government-wide efforts to accomplish this laundry list of tasks. Responding to a widespread sense that it had overpromised and underdelivered, and desperate to show its added value, S/CRS in summer 2006 narrowed its focus to three main areas: building interagency capacity; leading integrated strategies; and deploying to the field.

The Outside Role of the Pentagon

As the State Department grapples with its new mission, the Department of Defense (DoD) has embarked on a set of doctrinal and institutional innovations of its own. Stung by difficulties in Iraq, the Pentagon in early 2004 commissioned the Defense Science Board to undertake a study on the department's role in "the transition to and from hostilities."[57] This effort culminated in a lengthy report recommending, among other things, that DoD devote greater attention and resources to the requirements of post-conflict stabilization and reconstruction and be willing to use resources to strengthen the capabilities of civilian partner agencies. In autumn 2005, Secretary of Defense Donald Rumsfeld endorsed most of the recommendations in a new Pentagon Directive (3000.05) that for the first time established stability operations as a core mission for the DoD.[58]

Rather than create specialized divisions dedicated to stabilization and reconstruction operations, the directive mandates training in stability operations across the military. The directive also mandates that each US war plan include a detailed annex to explain how stabilization and reconstruction will occur. The Pentagon named a deputy assistant secretary of defense to oversee implementation of the directive, created a Defense Reconstruction Support Office to sustain these efforts in the field, and appointed a senior director for stability operations in each Combatant Command. Importantly, the directive also calls on DoD to coordinate with S/CRS and other civilian agencies and to support civilian-military teams in the field. At the same time, the document notes that civilian leadership or even participation may be impossible in chaotic environs or when civilian capabilities are themselves lacking. Accordingly, it declares, "US military forces shall be prepared to perform all tasks necessary to establish or maintain order when civilians cannot do so," from rebuilding infrastructure to reforming security sector institutions to reviving the private sector to developing institutions of representative government. Indeed, frustrated by delays in building adequate reconstruction capabilities within civilian agencies, Pentagon officials are exploring the creation of a civilian cadre at DoD to perform such functions, akin to a colonial service.

The Pentagon directive is consistent with a recent—and problematic—expansion of DoD's role in implementing relief, reconstruction, and development. While the US military is frequently called upon during active hostilities, in most efforts aimed at post-conflict reconstruction and stabilization, primary reliance on US military forces to implement assistance is neither good development practice nor good public diplomacy. Among other things, it can encourage unsustainable, externally imposed interventions.

One ambiguity in the US approach to stability and reconstruction operations is the question of which department, ultimately, should be in charge of directing these efforts. At first glance, National Security Presidential Directive 44 (NSPD 44) would appear to place the State Department (and by extension S/CRS) in the position of coordinating the involvement of all US government agencies, including DoD. A closer look suggests a more ambiguous relationship. There is no formal linkage between NSPD 44 and DoD Directive 3000.05, beyond the declaration that the

Pentagon will provide capabilities to support the post-conflict operations of civilian agencies, as appropriate. This ambiguity—as well as the lack of a State Department plan to implement NSPD 44—has complicated progress on a unified US approach to stabilization and reconstruction missions.

USAID: Down but Not Out

As a subcabinet agency whose administrator reports directly to the Secretary of State, USAID lacks the independence of either the Department of State or the Department of Defense to develop its own policy on stabilization and reconstruction. Nevertheless, it has been at the forefront of civilian involvement in such operations, playing a prominent role in Afghanistan and Iraq. In the interest of greater coordination with the US armed forces on development issues, particularly in post-conflict operations, USAID in March 2005 created a new Office of Military Affairs (OMA), designed to foster mutual understanding of the mandates and operational requirements of two very different implementing actors in the field. The office is intended to improve communication, advance joint doctrine and planning, and facilitate joint education, training, and the conduct of joint operations.

The Need for Better Interagency Coordination in Washington and the Field

To date, policy coherence in post-conflict operations has been hobbled by a lack of clear leadership among US government agencies. Notwithstanding the ostensible authority provided by NSPD 44, the S/CRS experience reaffirms a Washington truism: it is difficult to coordinate the entire US government from any one department, even with a staff drawn from multiple agencies. This is doubly true when the office in question has not been given resources adequate to command broad respect as a serious player capable of getting things done. It is even more challenging when the office has not been empowered to exert authority even within its own building. To overcome ambiguity, the National Security Council will need to play a more assertive role in post-conflict operations. The NSC, after all, is the only entity that possesses clear presidential authority to direct and coordinate all executive branch departments. Besides leading interagency task forces with S/CRS, the NSC should help that office develop doctrine that defines roles and responsibilities across agencies, military and civilian alike, as well the objectives in any prospective preventive or post-conflict effort. In parallel fashion, it is incumbent on the Secretary of State to reaffirm the primacy of S/CRS within the State Department itself, where there has been intense bureaucratic resistance and infighting, particularly from regional bureaus, for leadership in conflict prevention and post-conflict response. The creation of the Director of Foreign Assistance (DFA) position (discussed below) has further clouded the question of leadership within the State Department. During the summer of 2006, for example, the DFA insisted on coordinating US support for the reconstruction of Lebanon, despite S/CRS's clear mandate in this arena.

Better coordination in Washington must be complemented by clear roles and responsibilities in the field. During peacetime, the lines of authority over US government personnel in foreign countries are straightforward: the ambassador heads the country team and is supreme during crises, even though the military and civilians have their own reporting lines back to their departments. During military operations, things become more complicated, since US military forces report back via the secretary of defense to the president, outside the ambassadorial chain of command. Where disagreements arise, as frequently occurred during the tenure of the Coalition Provisional Authority in Iraq—there is no clear means to adjudicate their differences. Absent changes in legislation, the White House will need to clarify lines and phases of authority.

Improving Civilian-Military Planning

A central lesson of Iraq and Afghanistan is that civilian agencies must also develop new ways of planning, as well as integrated mechanisms for joint civil-military planning. Today, most "planning" in the State Department is ad hoc and conceptual, intended to develop a common understanding of the objective itself rather than to provide a roadmap detailing operations. The same tends to be true of USAID, although the latter does have experience in supervising the implementation of actual programs and projects. By contrast, a culture of operational planning permeates the US military, focusing on how to "get the job done" by melding overall strategy, doctrine, resources, and logistics into a coherent effort. Achieving greater policy coherence requires bridging these two planning cultures, so that the strategic determination of overall objectives, informed by a sophisticated understanding of local political and cultural environments, is accompanied by a more rigorous operational planning ethos along military lines, including regular testing, honing, and correction of plans through gaming, training, and exercises. In addition, the US government needs to embrace joint civilian-military planning whenever US forces may be used. Given the ramifications of military decisions on post-conflict operations, a truly joint approach would integrate civilian agency input into *all* phases of military involvement, rather than being tacked onto the post-conflict phase. In an initial effort to address this challenge, S/CRS has been working with Joint Forces Command to develop a common doctrine for stabilization and reconstruction operations that can facilitate detailed civil-military planning, as well as procedures for the deployment of civilian agency representatives to each Regional Combatant Command.

Building Standing Civilian Surge Capacity

One of the main disappointments to date has been the slowness of the United States in developing a cadre of qualified civilian personnel who can be deployed rapidly to the field in significant numbers to make a difference on the ground. The S/CRS office has been seeking to develop such capabilities in three concentric circles: (a) "first responders" within the State Department itself, embodied in a 100-person Active Response Corps (ARC) prepared to deploy at a moment's notice, backed by a 500-person Ready Reserve available over a slightly longer time horizon;[59] (b) enhanced technical capabilities within more specialized agencies of the US government, including USAID, the Department of Justice, and others; and (c) expertise from outside government, through standing arrangements with private contractors and NGOs, the creation of ready rosters of technical experts, and a potential Civilian Reserve Corps permitting qualified citizens to serve as temporary federal employees in field deployments.

Developing these human resources has proven painfully slow. Although the ARC is currently being formed, the full reserve will not be available until 2011. In the meantime, the State Department continues to have difficulty staffing a modest number of civilian slots in reconstruction efforts abroad, most notably Provincial Reconstruction Teams in Afghanistan and Iraq. Such a gap is likely to be filled only if the incentive structures of career promotions are changed to preferentially reward service in hardship environments, as well as joint service across agencies.[60] Finally, the department has made little headway in developing an actual civilian reserve. If current patterns persist, pressure will continue to grow for DoD to build up more civilian (as well as military) expeditionary capabilities of its own, akin to a colonial service. Such a step would be deeply problematic, increasing DoD's dominance in activities more appropriately conducted by civilian agencies.

Whole of Government in the Field? Provincial Reconstruction Teams

The most ambitious US effort to implement a joined-up approach to post-conflict operations has been the deployment of Provincial Reconstruction Teams (PRTs) to Afghanistan, and more recently to Iraq. PRTs were conceived in late 2002 as a way for the United States and its partners in Operation Enduring Freedom to deliver security, governance, and reconstruction assistance to Afghanistan, in the context of the "light footprint" adopted by the international community following the overthrow of the Taliban regime.[61] In the official US conception, the threefold mandate of PRTs has been to "improve security, extend the reach of the Afghan government, and facilitate reconstruction in priority provinces."[62] Although conceived as joint civilian-military units, US PRTs are overwhelmingly military in composition, with a handful of civilian officials among an average PRT size of perhaps 50-100 individuals.

Recent assessments by US government and independent

analysts suggest that PRTs have made positive, if modest, contributions to stability and reconstruction in various parts of Afghanistan, assisting in security sector reform, delivering useful resources, and facilitating dialogue among local actors and the central government. Nevertheless, the teams suffer from significant shortcomings.[63] First, the United States has developed no interagency doctrine for this joined-up approach to post-conflict operations, including a specification of the relative responsibilities of the military and civilian actors under this collaborative framework; nor has it invested in joint interagency training of PRT members prior to deployment, to ensure that civilian and military members are prepared for their mission. Second, the vast asymmetry between military and civilian components means that PRT activities have inevitably reflected military, rather than civilian, priorities.[64] This imbalance has been reinforced by the inability of civilian agencies, particularly State and USAID, to mobilize flexible, fast-disbursing funds, or to deploy adequate numbers of experienced personnel to fill even the small number of slots in the field (a problem compounded by rapid staff turnover). Third, many of the reconstruction projects undertaken by PRTs have been poor from a "development" perspective, dominated by unsustainable quick-impact projects. Unlike the UK in its own PRT deployments, the United States has conducted few interagency assessments of target provinces, leaving the activities and functions to be undertaken largely at the whim of the PRT commander. Too often, in the words of a joint interagency assessment, "schools were built without teachers and clinics without doctors."[65] Fourth, the use of US soldiers to perform "reconstruction" tasks has raised hackles from other aid providers, particularly international NGOs, who believe it has blurred the distinction between military and civilian spheres, contributed to the erosion of "humanitarian space," and led to the targeting of relief and development workers.[66] In the view of many critics, the primary responsibility of PRTs should be to provide the ambient security necessary to allow other actors—more skilled at the delivery of humanitarian and development assistance—to do their jobs.

Conflict Prevention

Although the United States has made progress in developing reconstruction and stabilization capabilities, it has taken few steps to prevent states from sliding into failure and violence in the first place. As a result, US engagement with weak states tends to be little more than a collection of independent, bilateral diplomatic, military, aid, trade, and financial relationships, shaped by the institutional mandates and bureaucratic priorities of respective agencies. Tentative efforts to prevent state failure and internal conflict have been isolated rather than mainstreamed. For example, USAID has cooperated with DoD in certain regional initiatives like the Trans-Saharan Counterterrorism Initiative. Similarly, S/CRS and the NSC now chair a low-level interagency working group on conflict management and mitigation. What is missing is a truly integrated strategy toward fragile states that brings all relevant tools of national power and influence to bear in the service of coherent country plans, one that can ensure alignment of the 3Ds, as well as other components of US engagement, not only in Washington but also at US embassies, within country teams under the direction of the ambassador. Foreign aid reform is an initial step in this direction, but by itself inadequate.

The fragmentation of the current US approach to fragile states reflects a lack of clear leadership and direction from the White House and particularly the National Security Council, which has failed to bring together the different departments in an effort to harmonize efforts and bridge differences. It also reflects unwillingness on the part of Congress to provide significant resources to sustain the diplomacy and development sides of the 3D triangle, whether in supporting institutional innovations like S/CRS, or providing aid to the dozens of fragile states besides Iraq and Afghanistan. Success in achieving a more integrated and balanced approach to fragile states will ultimately depend on greater direction and ownership from the president himself, who has remained oddly passive in the debates swirling around the interagency. It will also require legislative activism from the Congress, which—with the exception of the Senate Committee on Foreign Relations—has been largely missing in action in advancing this agenda in the past five years.

Choosing Where to Engage: Warning and Assessment

A greater commitment to prevention would require a more robust system for monitoring and early warning, linked with an authoritative mechanism to jump-start early action. One place to begin is by deepening intelligence collection and the analysis of the links between state weakness and specific threats to US national interests and international security. Such an early warning system could help policymakers determine where to devote US efforts and build up political will and interagency attention for preventive action. Currently, the State Department, DoD, and USAID each maintain their separate monitoring and warning processes to identify countries that might warrant intervention. Within the State Department, for example, S/CRS and the policy planning staff collaborate with the National Intelligence Council in generating a semiannual list of countries at risk of instability that might be the subject of contingency planning for conflict mitigation or potential intervention. Meanwhile, the Pentagon has instituted a separate process to "develop a list of countries and areas with the potential for US military intervention."[67] Likewise, the Conflict Management and Mitigation office at USAID has developed a Conflict Assessment Framework to assess and provide policy options for ameliorating violent conflict. While this proliferation may be inevitable, given distinct agency mandates, there needs to be some means of reconciling these lists. With this end in mind, S/CRS has promoted the use of a single interagency methodology to assess instability and conflict, designed to provide policymakers in different departments with a common understanding of conditions in potential crisis countries.

Foreign Aid Reform and US Fragile States Policy

Recent changes in US foreign assistance policy have some potential to foster a more integrated and strategic approach to stabilizing fragile states across the US government. In January 2006, Secretary of State Condoleezza Rice unveiled a major plan to reform US foreign aid architecture. The reform initiative is part of a larger "transformational diplomacy" agenda, intended to bolster democratic, well-governed states.[68] The core premise of this effort is that the main threats to the United States emanate today not from great powers but from the spillover effects of dysfunctional governance and economic stagnation in the developing world. To address these dangers, the United States must use all of its policy instruments, including foreign aid, to reform the domestic institutions and authority structures of other countries so that they are able and willing to exercise responsible sovereignty. The reform effort is the boldest step yet by the United States to align development and diplomacy.

The administration's reform plan aims to bring discipline to the highly fractured foreign aid regime, primarily by centralizing management and accountability over USAID and State Department funding, which currently pours out of eighteen distinct accounts (to say nothing of the twenty-odd other federal departments and agencies that maintain their own aid programs). The objective of the reform plan is to ensure that US foreign assistance responds to US strategic direction and priorities.

To oversee and implement such changes, Secretary Rice appointed Randall Tobias as the country's first Director of Foreign Assistance (DFA), serving simultaneously as administrator of USAID, at the level of deputy secretary of state. The DFA's primary duties are to oversee the drafting of an overall US government foreign assistance strategy, and the development of five-year integrated country plans and one-year operational plans in each country where the US operates. He has oversight and authority over all aid programs and funding of USAID and the Department of State.

In May 2006, Tobias released a new Strategic Framework for Foreign Assistance, explaining how the DFA would seek to rationalize foreign aid appropriated to the State Department and USAID. In support of the core goal of promoting "democratic, well-governed states," the framework establishes five overarching objectives for US foreign assistance: advancing peace and security; promoting just and democratic governance; encouraging investments in people; promoting economic growth; and providing humanitarian assistance. In parallel fashion, the Framework classifies all developing countries into five distinct categories, in each case establishing a general end goal and a "graduation trajectory," which may include moving up to the next category or graduating from foreign aid entirely. These categories include *rebuilding* countries (twelve countries emerging from internal or external conflict[69]); *developing* countries (sixty-six low- or lower-middle income countries that do not meet Millennium Challenge Account [MCA] performance criteria, or a hard hurdle on either corruption or political rights); *transforming* countries (twenty-four low- or lower-middle income countries that pass MCA performance criteria, as well as a hard democracy hurdle); *sustaining partnership* countries (forty-three middle-income or better countries "for which US support is provided to sustain partnerships, progress, and peace"); and *restrictive* countries (11 states of concern where there are significant governance issues, and where direct US funding is limited by statute or policy).[70]

The administration decided to implement the new framework in two phases. For the FY07 budget, more than sixty countries representing the lion's share of foreign aid were placed on a "fast track," with operational foreign aid plans drawn up to reflect their country classification. Beginning in FY08, all developing countries will have such plans. To support this work, the DFA will have an eighty to one hundred person office, with staff drawn primarily from State and USAID staff.

The administration's reforms have the potential to bring more discipline to the chaotic US foreign aid regime, by centralizing management and accountability over USAID and State Department funds. They also place a laudable emphasis on state-building, underlining the need to help build the institutions developing countries need to provide security, create conditions for growth, and govern effectively for their people. Nevertheless, the plan has several shortcomings.

Most obviously, the framework fails to articulate a coherent strategy for engaging the world's fifty-odd weak and failing states. For diplomatic reasons, the administration has not specified a fragile state category in its taxonomy of aid recipients, choosing instead to lump most of them into the large grab bag of "developing countries." This lacuna is inconsistent with the administration's espoused concern with weak and failing states. It suggests that the United States has a reactive policy toward war-torn countries, and a punitive one toward rogue states, while lacking a preventive strategy to stop struggling states from sliding toward either status. It is also problematic from a practical standpoint because (as the OECD/DAC has recognized) states that are unable or unwilling to provide essential political goods to their inhabitants present distinctive policy dilemmas for their donors. In the absence of a specific fragile states category, one hopes the administration will at least bear these unique needs in mind as it develops its country plans. At the very least, these plans should incorporate USAID's common principles for engaging in fragile states. This review of current programs could also explore a reallocation of aid toward fragile states, where conditions permit, since only a tiny portion of US foreign assistance currently goes to advance stability and development in fragile states.

Equally problematic, the actual power of the coordinator to impose coherence is heavily circumscribed. Tobias has direct authority only over USAID and State Department funds, but even here he is likely to face congressional resistance to shifting funds across separate accounts. The DFA will also continue to be constrained by the plague of legislative and executive branch earmarks on the foreign assistance budget, which undercut aid effectiveness. In addition, the coordinator will have direct budgetary authority only over State and USAID funds, leaving nearly half of US foreign assistance—some 45 percent—outside of his purview. This includes the Millennium Challenge Account, HIV/AIDS spending, as well as the aid initiatives of multiple domestic US agencies, including the departments of Agriculture, Energy, Health and Human Services, Labor, and Treasury, some of which are quite large.[71] Nor does the DFA have any control over the burgeoning assistance programs of the Department of Defense, one of the most striking trends in recent US foreign aid policy. In 2006, the Pentagon controlled nearly a fifth of total US foreign aid, particularly in the fields of post-conflict reconstruction, counter-terrorism, counternarcotics, and humanitarian assistance.[72]

Yet even the figure of 55 percent exaggerates the DFA's actual scope of action. Much of the aid ostensibly under his purview is effectively off-limits to any reallocation, because it goes to a handful of strategic countries, including Israel, Egypt, Iraq, Pakistan, Colombia, and Jordan. It is fair to ask what sort of "transformation" the DFA can accomplish in the face of such constraints.

Beyond these obstacles, there is a danger that the reform plan will result not in true strategic direction and coherence but in business as usual budgeting. Early indications from the first DFA-chaired country coordination meetings have not been promising. Rather than engaging in a rigorous assessment of how aid should be allocated to achieve the five main strategic goals, participants in some instances have simply mapped current agency budgets over the new strategic framework, shoe-horning current programs and activities into the new aid categories. Whether the DFA will be able to overcome such bureaucratic resistance remains to be seen.

Finally, it remains unclear how the DFA plans to define "success" across its five core objectives, or what indicators it will use to monitor and evaluate progress in achieving them. The initial metrics proposed by the DFA largely measure inputs and outputs—the number of programs implemented or amount of money spent—and not outcomes—the relative impact of inputs. One solution to this perennial challenge of honest impact assessment would be to create an independent monitoring and evaluation unit.

Funding: All Sword, No Ploughshare?

An effective US approach to fragile states will require not only a strategy that integrates various agencies, but also sufficient resources to make a tangible difference on the ground. Perhaps the biggest obstacle to a whole of government approach to failed states is the massive budgetary imbalance between the Department of Defense and US civilian agencies, which leaves the United States ill-prepared to address the long-term challenge of weak governance and chronic poverty in the developing world. Notwithstanding a significant increase in overall US foreign assistance over the past several years, the federal budget remains heavily skewed toward military expenditures, shortchanging critical civilian investments in state-building. At the aggregate level, US defense spending (some $578 billion in FY07 requests) outpaces civilian dimensions of US global engagement (some $35 billion) by a factor of seventeen to one. Of this latter amount, foreign assistance represents nearly $24 billion, or less than 1 percent of the federal budget. This misalignment deprives civilian agencies of the resources they need to build up their own technical expertise and response capabilities, respond to unforeseen contingencies, and provide critical foreign aid to fragile and post-conflict states. A case in point is the repeated failure of S/CRS to secure a modest $100 million Conflict Response Fund for contingency operations. Besides exaggerating the position of the Pentagon in the nation's national security structure, current budgetary allocations lead to an overreliance on soldiers to conduct post-conflict activities, from policing to infrastructure, which should more appropriately be done by civilian agencies and actors.[73]

While the Bush administration has given unprecedented rhetorical emphasis to weak and failing states, the actual proportion of US foreign assistance budget that actually goes to support institution building in fragile states remains modest. By one estimate, if we subtract spending on Iraq, Afghanistan, and Pakistan, and expenditures on HIV/AIDS, the administration's proposed US bilateral assistance for FY07 amounts to little more than one dollar per person per year in the world's fifty weakest countries.[74] While spending aid effectively in fragile states can be extremely challenging, current budgetary requests are inadequate compared with the magnitude of the task.

Perhaps the biggest structural obstacle to a more balanced budget for fragile states is the committee structure in Congress, which involves separate authorization and appropriations committees for the State Department and USAID, on the one hand, and the US military on the other. As long as civilian agencies and the Pentagon continue to be funded from different budgets rather than from pooled accounts (as in the UK) or even in a single national security budget, they will have little incentive to formulate those budgets in common and lobby for each others' priorities. Unfortunately, there is little interest in Congress in reforming committee structures to improve coordination across jurisdictional lines. Moreover, the limited Congressional appetite for nation-building is likely to dwindle for the foreseeable future, in light of the ongoing difficulties in stabilizing postwar Iraq, and the looming budget crunch on Capitol Hill.

Conclusion

Improved US performance in prevention, crisis response, and the long-term process of "state-building" after conflict will require a more integrated approach that goes well beyond impressive military instruments, to include major investments in critical civilian capabilities. Necessary ingredients include embracing prevention as an operating principle; achieving a common strategic vision about the goals of US action; establishing criteria and methods for determining where to engage; clarifying interagency leadership within Washington and in the field; improving civil-military planning and coordination; developing a standing civilian surge capacity and relevant technical skills; and providing significantly higher funding for civilian engagement with failing and post-conflict states. Based on the experience of the US military, achieving greater "jointness" in US policy toward fragile states may well take years, if not decades. Reconciling the conflicting cultures, mandates, operating procedures, and time horizons of US government departments and agencies will be a recurrent challenge.

Chapter Three

Canada

Overview

Whole of government rhetoric toward fragile states is strongly embraced across the various agencies of the Canadian government, and especially those that make up the 3Ds: the Department of National Defense (DND), Department for Foreign Affairs and International Trade (DFAIT), and the Canadian International Development Agency (CIDA). Policymakers in Ottawa recognize the need for holistic approaches that can simultaneously address the security, governance, social, and economic needs of fragile states and nurture the emergence of indigenous institutions capable of providing these goods. The rationale for such an approach is spelled out in Canada's *International Policy Statement* (IPS) of 2005, which calls for greater interdepartmental coordination in addressing a wide range of challenges to global peace and security, including "the unique development and security challenges posed by poorly performing, unstable and conflict-ridden countries."[75]

Canadians have already attained a good level of interagency coordination, reflecting in part the generally collegial, collaborative ethos that permeates the Canadian government. Ottawa established a permanent interagency Stabilization and Reconstruction Task Force (START), housed within DFAIT, with a broad mandate and dedicated funding to work on issues of conflict prevention, disaster response, and post-conflict reconstruction. It has also espoused the importance of whole of government approaches in its strategies and activities in Afghanistan, Haiti, and

Sudan, and it has contributed strongly to multilateral efforts to address fragile states, including within the OECD/DAC and the UN. The Canadian government warmly embraced the logic of the UN High-Level Panel Report of 2004, which underlined the importance of effective sovereign states as the cornerstone of world order in the twenty-first century.[76] Despite the January 2006 election of Canada's first Conservative government in twelve years, this political commitment to working bilaterally and multilaterally on issues surrounding the fragile states agenda continues to prevail.

Nevertheless, Canada continues to struggle in achieving cross-departmental agreement on objectives and motivations for its interventions, as well as in designing and implementing country strategies. The START unit, while more successful than its US counterpart in operationalizing its mandate, has struggled to assert its coordinating leadership in conflict prevention and post-conflict reconstruction, having to contend with bureaucratic turf battles and departmental preferences for template-driven, stove-piped programs. Furthermore, the government remains unsure about where and how to devote its foreign aid to fragile states.

Origins of Canadian Interest

In contrast to the experience of the United States, Canada's policy interest in weak and failing states is not simply an artifact of 9/11. Rather, it builds upon a venerable Canadian tradition of international engagement in advancing global security and development. This legacy includes a longtime leadership in UN peacekeeping; the promotion of concepts of human security and peacebuilding (under former Foreign Minister Lloyd Axworthy); mobilization of the international campaign to ban land mines; and the establishment of the International Commission on Intervention and State Sovereignty, which created and led to the promotion of the international "responsibility to protect" agenda. Other landmarks in this trend include the creation of a Peacebuilding Fund in CIDA in 1997, and a Human Security Program within DFAIT in 2000.[77] Canada was also a leader in helping to draft the OECD/DAC *Guidelines on Conflict, Peace, and Development Cooperation.*[78]

Canadian interest in more integrated policy responses toward fragile and post-conflict states reflects in large measure the perceived lessons of peace operations during the 1990s, particularly in the Balkans and Africa, which highlighted the limitations of uncoordinated approaches to security, governance, and development in war-torn societies. These experiences persuaded Canadian government officials that the international community lacked adequate arrangements to address recurrent challenges falling between conventional peacekeeping, on the one hand, and traditional development, on the other, particularly in areas like the rule of law, policing, judicial and security sector reform, and transitional administration. Rather than continually reinventing the wheel and scrambling for resources to confront each new contingency, Canada and other donor governments needed standing civilian capabilities and fast-disbursing, flexible resources to respond with alacrity in fluid environments. More broadly, Canada needed new approaches to conflict prevention and peace building that could unite the defense, development, and diplomatic communities in addressing the root causes of state fragility and conflict. These conclusions would be reinforced by subsequent Canadian experiences in Haiti, Afghanistan, Sudan, and elsewhere.

The attacks of September 11, 2001, propelled Canada's attention to fragile states into higher gear, by underscoring the linkage between development and security, and underlining the need for a more integrated approach to preventing state failure and conducting post-conflict operations. From CIDA's perspective, the message was that in many contexts physical security is a fundamental precondition for poverty reduction. For DFAIT and DND, it was that sustainable livelihoods and good governance were important antidotes to political instability and violent extremism—and that building effective institutions in precarious states would help ensure that transnational threats never reached North America. Any effective policy response to these interdependent challenges would require a more collaborative response among agencies that could draw upon their comparative advantages.

Canada's International Policy Statement

The foundation for an integrated Canadian approach to weak and failing states was spelled out in the country's *International Policy Statement* (IPS) of April 2005, produced under the Liberal Government of Paul Martin. The product of a laborious interdepartmental drafting process, the IPS is an ambitious attempt to establish the priorities and parameters of Canada's global engagement in the twenty-first century, with an eye toward harmonizing the roles of DFAIT, DND, and CIDA in the achievement of Canada's national objectives. The IPS declares the government's intention to devote an additional C$17 billion a year toward national defense; to expand its diplomatic presence overseas; and to increase development assistance to focus on specific countries of concern. The document is premised on the assumption that Canada's own security and prosperity are increasingly linked to peace and development abroad, and furthermore, that today's global challenges can only be addressed through vigorous multilateral cooperation, as well as engagement with civil society.

A central theme of the IPS is the imperative of adopting a whole of government approach to pressing global challenges, including fragile states, both in Ottawa and in the field. Although the IPS endorses expanded Canadian post-conflict response capabilities, it places even more emphasis on steps to anticipate and prevent conflict in the world's poor, underdeveloped, and insecure countries. It particularly stresses the need to build effective states so as to prevent the spread of transnational security threats.[79] Although the IPS was drafted and approved under its Liberal predecessor, the Conservative government of Prime Minister Stephen Harper has endorsed this document, committing Canada to whole of government responses to fragile states and state-building, albeit with more emphasis on freedom, democracy, and human rights.[80]

A Common Canadian Approach toward Fragile States?

In principle, the IPS should provide an authoritative basis for developing a whole of government approach to fragile and post-conflict states. In practice, the document's painful gestation testifies to the difficulty of getting interagency buy-in on an overriding principle of how and why Canada should be engaged around the globe.[81] While the IPS is to be lauded for bringing the issue of fragile states firmly onto the Canadian foreign policy agenda, and for calling for the establishment of a permanent stabilization and reconstruction task force, a glaring omission in IPS "whole of government" rhetoric is an established definition or classification for fragile states, let alone an interagency wide strategy toward assessing state fragility and the launching of policy interventions in these countries.

During winter 2006, the Canadian government began the laborious process of groping toward such an interdepartmental strategy, building off a November 2005 document from CIDA, *On the Road to Recovery: Breaking the Cycle of Poverty and Fragility—Guidelines for Effective Development Cooperation in Fragile States.*[82] By late spring 2006, following inputs from DFAIT, DND, CIDA, and the Privy Council Office (PCO), this process had culminated in a draft for consideration, defining the importance of fragile states in Canadian global engagement, and spelling out how the government intends to identify fragile states, respond on the basis of joint needs assessment and conflict analyses, and forge interagency collaboration in specific situations. As of January 2007, the document was still in draft form. The government hoped to complete it but had not yet decided whether the strategy would actually culminate in a public document outlining Canada's joined-up response to fragile states.

Whether or not a public document is ever released, one can make several observations about the general Canadian approach to fragile states. First, Ottawa recognizes that whole of government efforts should put primary emphasis on state-building—or nurturing the emergence of a legitimate and accountable state that can deliver essential goods to its people. Second, Canadian officials acknowledge that any whole of government effort must adapt to the underlying roots of fragility and conflict within the specific country in question. While certain general principles of engagement may apply, there can be no "cookie-cutter" approach to Canada's response. Third, Ottawa's conception of "whole of government" runs well beyond the 3Ds, to include a range of technical and primarily domestic agencies such as the Department of Justice, Elections Canada, The Royal Canadian Mounted Police

(RCMP), Finance Canada, and the Department of Public Safety and Emergency Preparedness (PSEP).

Fourth, Canadian policymakers recognize that a whole of government approach to fragile states need not imply an equal role among all of the agencies involved. The level of involvement by DND, for example, may vary widely with context—being heavy in Afghanistan, say, but limited in Haiti. Likewise, in Iraq, CIDA is spending hundreds of millions of dollars on reconstruction efforts, whereas DND is contributing little as a matter of Canadian policy. What is critical is not that each agency's contribution be roughly proportional but that interventions be informed by whole of government principles—even when some departments are more out in front than others—and that involvement is sufficiently flexible to ramp various components up (or down) as circumstances change. Moreover, Canadian officials recognize that in multinational operations, an integrated or 3D approach in the field may actually include representatives from separate donor governments, for example, with development officials from one country collaborating with diplomatic or military actors from another.

Perspectives from the Canadian Defense, Diplomatic, and Development Agencies

Overall, Canada's prospects for achieving a harmonious whole of government approach to fragile states are enhanced by the relatively balanced nature of power among the three most relevant ministries. Unlike the United States, Canada lacks an outsize defense department with colossal resources and commensurate weight in policy decisions. Indeed, the global footprint of the Canadian armed forces is perhaps two orders of magnitude smaller than that of its US counterpart, with the largest deployment, by far, in Afghanistan, where Canada currently maintains approximately 2,300 troops in NATO's International Security Assistance Force (ISAF) mission.[83] Furthermore, the importance of interagency cooperation has been explicitly endorsed in the IPS, and tentative steps have been taken to create formalized interagency task forces and funding mechanisms devoted to civilian activities in fragile and post-conflict states. While there is very strong support for government-wide cooperation, some fear that enhanced coordination may blur lines of responsibility and operational activities. There have also been concerns to ensure that whole of government approaches do not lead to a homogenization of distinct departmental concerns, violate the mandates of any of them, or reduce their comparative advantages.

Canada's Department of National Defense (DND) has long been comfortable collaborating with civilian agencies. However, its interest in whole of government responses to failed and failing states increased dramatically after 9/11. DND recognizes the importance of working with—and not at cross purposes with—CIDA and DFAIT in such countries, as well as consulting and sharing information with START. This is true even in highly militarized environments, particularly in Afghanistan, where DND tends to engage DFAIT and CIDA as equals.[84] Compared to its US counterpart, DND is less preoccupied with the global war on terror and with counterinsurgency efforts, and more attuned to requirements of peacekeeping and stability operations. This orientation facilitates alignment and cooperation with civilian departments.

DFAIT has also embraced joined-up approaches to working in unstable climates, viewing failed and fragile states as a key challenge to Canadian peace and security. The IPS particularly emphasizes the importance of conflict prevention, "through development strategies, support for human rights and democracy, diplomacy to prevent conflict and contributions to build human security."[85] At the same time, experiences in Afghanistan and elsewhere persuaded DFAIT that CIDA, in particular, lacked the mandate, authority, and skill sets to help bridge the gap between immediate security tasks undertaken by DND, and longer-term capacity building and poverty reduction measures. While CIDA has long worked in fragile states, its engagement has been restricted mainly to ODA-eligible activities, as defined by the OECD/DAC, which preclude the agency from mobilizing resources for a range of transitional activities deemed necessary to establish stability, and law and order in volatile environments. Moreover, CIDA does not have all the necessary professional expertise and resources to devote to interdepartmental coordination in hard security matters like police deployments, transitional justice, peace support operation activities, and other similar politically charged initiatives.

In response to these perceived gaps, the Canadian government established the Stabilization and Reconstruction Task Force (START) and placed it within DFAIT. The office (discussed in greater detail below) is intended to permit the Canadian government to respond quickly to crises, as well as to give the foreign affairs department the independent resources needed to enhance its operational activity.

Like other bilateral aid agencies, CIDA continues to focus primarily on development cooperation initiatives as defined by the DAC. The 2005 International Policy Statement establishes five main focus areas for CIDA: education, environment, good governance, health and HIV/AIDS, and private sector development (as well as one crosscutting issue, gender equality). In a departure from tradition, CIDA has recently become more selective in its choice of development cooperation partners, choosing to focus the bulk of its aid resources on just 25 countries, selected on the basis of their poverty levels, their ability to use aid effectively, and Canada's perceived comparative advantage in being able to make a significant contribution to their development.[86] Canada has committed to doubling its ODA between 2001 and 2010.

At the same time, CIDA is increasingly aware that working on fragile states is a growing part of its core business: Indeed, the development agency claims that it is already spending nearly C$500 million operating in fragile states around the world (a large proportion of this in Iraq). As noted in its November 2005 document, *On the Road to Recovery: Breaking the Cycle of Poverty and Fragility—Guidelines for Effective Development Cooperation in Fragile States*, CIDA believes that fragile states present unique development challenges that go far beyond its conventional sector-based approach, requiring new forms of cooperation with other government departments and the international community—whose priorities in both cases will naturally diverge from CIDA's. To address the root sources of fragility and to provide a platform for other departments and international partners to collaborate, the document envisions whole of government strategies based on three interlocking circles: security and stability; good governance; and livelihoods. The ultimate objective is to leverage cooperation among different agencies—and to avoid a pathological pattern of redundancy and incoherence that would arise if each agency simply went its own way in approaching these problems.

For CIDA, the central implication is that progress in fragile states requires greater collaboration with outside "enablers," for example with the DND and RCMP on security sector reform, and with DFAIT on providing the necessary diplomatic support for the effective implementation of complex, politically sensitive projects, ranging from voluntary disarmament to governance reform. The specific basket of activities in each circle—and the role of Canadian government departments in designing and implementing them—is determined by context, opportunities, comparative advantages, and past track record of engagements, as well as whether the country in question is failing, failed, or recovering.

Canada's quest for strategic integration has not always gone smoothly. CIDA, in addition to engaging in fragile states and using "nontraditional" types of development aid, has felt pressure since 9/11 to engage in initiatives that it perceives as lying outside of its institutional mandate, for instance by contributing to Canada's Counter-Terrorism Capacity Building Program. It has resisted, on the grounds that while this program is perhaps important for Canadian security, it does little to advance poverty reduction in the developing world. For its own part, CIDA has pushed other agencies for a stronger Canadian commitment to policy coherence for development (as opposed to solely for national security).

CIDA is generally able to resist pressure from other agencies seeking to exploit its resources, thanks in part to the aforementioned commitment by the previous Liberal government (embraced by its successor) to spend two-thirds of its bilateral assistance on its twenty-five poor development cooperation partners. This commitment, as well as Canada's promise to double aid to sub-Saharan Africa, places constraints on efforts by other departments to argue for shifts in aid allocations to specific fragile states. Where Canadian aid has been devoted to fragile states, it goes almost exclusively to five key target countries: Iraq, Afghanistan, Palestine, Haiti, and Sudan. Canada's decision to devote most of the remaining aid to relatively good performers raises questions of whether its policy exacerbates the problem of "aid orphans." It also limits CIDA's ability to accomplish anything concrete in the vast share of fragile states. During summer 2006, the Privy Council Office began to push CIDA to engage more frequently in poorly performing fragile states.

Interdepartmental Policy Coordination: START

Policy coordination within the Canadian government takes place at several levels. The Privy Council Office (PCO) fills a critical role in communicating to departments the prime minister's political priorities, and reciprocally, in keeping the PM informed of divergent perspectives within those departments. The Cabinet's Foreign Affairs and National Security Committee (FANS) is charged with ensuring that departments integrate their broad strategies and approaches to specific issues in the realms of foreign, defense, development, and trade policy, as well as with supervising the International Assistance Envelope that funds much of Canada's engagement in these areas. The policy recommendations that FANS sends to the Cabinet are typically based on position papers (memoranda to cabinet) produced by interdepartmental committees at the level of deputy or assistant deputy minister, as well as more ad hoc working groups, chaired in both cases by DFAIT, which has the lead within the government in coordinating Canada's international engagement.

The main institutional innovation created by the Canadian government to address coordination challenges in fragile states is the Stabilization and Reconstruction Task Force (START), which was mandated by the International Policy Statement. START is a standing interagency mechanism located within DFAIT that is intended to provide a platform for prompt, government-wide response to the challenges of preventing and responding to crises, including coordination of military and civilian activities in post-conflict operations.

START has a broad remit—indeed, broader than a similar office in the United States, the Office of the Coordinator for Reconstruction and Stabilization (S/CRS). It is designed to address a range of crises and challenges, as reflected in the titles of its four directorates: humanitarian affairs and natural disasters; peacekeeping and operations; conflict prevention and peacebuilding; and landmines and small arms. Its mandate includes both reaction—ensuring greater coherence and coordination across government in post-conflict operations and humanitarian assistance—and prevention—looking ahead to head off incipient crises.

In contrast to the United States or the United Kingdom, which attempted to create new conflict response capabilities (S/CRS and the PCRU) out of whole cloth, the Canadian government made a conscious choice to build on existing capacities, personnel, and units when creating START. This decision helped moderate some of the predictable bureaucratic resistance to the office, as well as allowing it to build on existing capabilities. The office also inherited as part of its initial work stream several high profile countries in which Canada was already heavily engaged, including Afghanistan, Haiti, Sudan, Iraq, and the Palestinian territories. START has also led Canadian involvement in disaster relief, including leading the government of Canada's response to the Pakistan earthquake. It also funds CANADEM, a nongovernmental organization that maintains a roster of some 5,000 Canadians with particular skill sets that might be useful in fragile and post-conflict environments, including performing election monitoring or fulfilling police functions.

START is an important addition to the Canadian foreign policy toolbox, providing for the first time an interdepartmental focal point for dealing with multiple contingencies. Critically, the office has access to independent resources, in the form of the C$100 million a year Global Peace and Security Fund (GPSF) to facilitate rapid response, so that (unlike the past) DFAIT does not need to approach CIDA (or DND) to beg for funds. These resources are essential to jump-starting rapid response to crises, and getting other agencies to the table. The office will build up to seventy-five personnel (at the time of this writing it housed approximately sixty Canadian officials).

Despite its potential, START faces significant hurdles in fulfilling its ambitious mandate. To begin with, its placement within DFAIT, while logical in some respects, has been problematic from the point of view of interagency coordination. From the beginning, there has been debate over how much control the START office should have in actually directing Canadian involvement in crisis countries. The initial notion within DFAIT was that START could serve as the locus for government-wide policy making to prevent and respond to conflict and disasters. This gambit generated predictable resistance from other departments, particularly CIDA and DND, which contended that giving START explicit authority over the entire government would violate the principle of ministerial accountability. Accordingly, the Cabinet created a START Advisory Board, composed of representatives from a broad range of government departments, as well as from the Privy Council Office (PCO), with a mandate to endorse its activities, and, when necessary, send issues for decision and adjudication to the ministerial level. The head of START chairs the Advisory Board, but decisions are taken on the basis of consensus.

In addition, staffing of the START office remains an issue. Although it is supposed to include colleagues seconded from the various agencies including CIDA, DND, and DFAIT, so far its staff has been drawn overwhelmingly from the foreign ministry—a worrisome development, since one aim of detailing individuals from across the various agencies is to expose these departments to different mentalities. Even when seconding staff to START, moreover, home departments have tended to regard the office more as a creature of DFAIT than a genuine interagency body. Furthermore, the co-location of officials from 3D departments presupposes that information will be shared on a regular basis and that analysis and planning will be done in an integrated fashion. This is not yet happening, unfortunately.

In assessing START's practical impact, most of those interviewed believed that it had been most successful in creating a new, more flexible funding structure to finance activities that CIDA may not have been able to fund (due to its ODA guidelines), that DFAIT may not have had the capability of to make operational, and that DND may not have had the desire to undertake in view of its military mandate. START and its Advisory Board have also strengthened coordination among the different agencies, particularly in high-profile or crisis situations. START has found it more difficult to generate consensus on objectives, as well as interdepartmental coordination, in the conflict prevention and peacebuilding phases, where bureaucratic turf battles and stove-piped patterns tend to reassert themselves.

On the other hand, it appears that incentives have not been great enough to create unified, coherent, and (critically) creative strategies for operating in fragile states. As interviewees noted, there are few professional rewards for pursuing interdepartmental coordination, and joint approaches to long-term institution building in fragile states are often overwhelmed by pressures within single agencies to demonstrate quick results, including moving money. While there is little inherent resistance to collaboration among working-level officers, the time pressures set by senior management rarely allow for adequate whole of government consultation and planning.

In addition, some staff at CIDA view START with trepidation, fearing that the GPSF may undermine existing coherence among departments by sponsoring small, stand-alone initiatives that do not fit within broader interdepartmental commitments, as well as raising expectations for long-term engagement that CIDA is not prepared or suited to follow. CIDA wishes to educate DFAIT on development-related matters but is uncomfortable with DFAIT's use of a conflict fund for development purposes (as in the health interventions in Aceh, for example). The danger is that such funding streams will create turf battles, rather than productive and collaborative divisions of labor. To justify itself, these critics believe, the GPSF should bring a qualitative change to the way the government actually engages in fragile states, and not just replicate a project-based approach that CIDA or even DND could do. The GSPF should allow START to develop and implement joint integrated programs, while increasing Canadian policy influence in recipient governments.

In addition to START, two other specialized mechanisms to coordinate Canada's response to fragile states deserve mention:

Canada Corps and the Canadian Police Arrangement (CPA). Canada Corps, which was mandated by the IPS and is housed within CIDA, seeks to mobilize Canadians with expertise in key pillars of governance (human rights, rule of law, democratization, public sector institutions, and conflict prevention and peacebuilding) for deployment to war-torn and fragile states. The CPA is a specialized interdepartmental coordination mechanism—involving DFAIT, RCMP, CIDA, and PSEP (as well as DOJ and DND on an ad hoc basis)— that is charged with mobilizing, preparing, and deploying civilian police components of international peace operations.

Devising Country Strategies

One of the most important innovations in Canada's approach to fragile states—indeed for all nations—is the requirement that the ambassador or high commissioner, in consultation with home departments in Ottawa, outline an integrated approach to Canada's engagement with the host nation. Starting in 2006, each ambassador (or high commissioner) must annually develop a "Country Strategy" setting out how the embassy—which may include representatives of a dozen or more Canadian departments and agencies—intends to advance Canada's interests. The goal is to hold the ambassador accountable for fostering a whole of government approach, principally through linking the program with the ambassador's Performance Management Agreement. These country strategies now cover roughly 90 percent of the globe. Interview subjects suggest that increased embassy leadership in formulating country strategies holds great promise for enhancing the coherence of Canadian policy in fragile states. Their main drawback is that they tend to focus on a short time horizon—the upcoming year.

When a country in crisis is deemed particularly important to Canadian interests, there is generally a move to create an interdepartmental task force, which is increasingly chaired by START. The focus of these meetings has thus far tended to be less on civil-military planning processes (of which DND in particular is skeptical) than on coming up with a shared understanding of the situation and a pragmatic consensus on the objectives and motivations for Canadian engagement.

The three main field locations for Canada's whole of government strategies and efforts in fragile states have been in Afghanistan, Haiti, and Sudan. Afghanistan is the site of Canada's most significant military presence by far, with 2,300 troops. In addition, Canada leads a Provincial Reconstruction Team in Kandahar, explicitly designed with whole of government principles in mind. Beyond its military component, it includes a DFAIT official, a CIDA representative, and six members of the RCMP. In contrast to the situation in Afghanistan, DND is almost totally absent in Haiti, where DFAIT and CIDA work closely. START is spending some C$15 million in Haiti, with CIDA spending a considerable amount more on police and rule of law, a program implemented in part by the RCMP. Finally, Canada is planning a whole of government strategy for Sudan, incorporating the defense, development, and diplomacy communities within the Canadian government.

While Canadian officials attribute the relative smoothness in country coordination efforts to the informality and collegiality of interdepartmental relations, particularly compared to recent US experience, there is a sense that greater strategic thinking could be done to incorporate the specific issues of state fragility into Canadian engagement as well as to encourage more sustained and genuine interdepartmental cooperation in these states of concern.

Financial Instruments

Canada's foreign aid resources, collectively known as the International Assistance Envelope, are comprised of five distinct funding windows: (1) support for international financial institutions, supervised by the Ministry of Finance; (2) aid for development, supervised by CIDA; (3) resources to respond to unanticipated crises, in the form of a C$150 million Crisis Pool, on which both CIDA and DFAIT can bid; (4) funds for peace and security, in the form of the C$100 million Global Peace and Security Fund (GPSF) supervised by the START office; and (5) resources for development research.

As noted earlier, CIDA, which controls the lion's share of Canada's bilateral assistance, is mandated by law to direct two-thirds of its entire aid to some twenty-five focus countries, with the additional proviso that half of all Canadian ODA go to African countries (with an annual increase of 8 percent). There are thus significant constraints on what CIDA can spend on fragile states, outside of the "fragile 5" of Iraq, Afghanistan, Palestine, Haiti, and Sudan.

The creation of the Crisis Pool and the Global Peace and Security Fund both reflect awareness that Canada requires flexible financing arrangements that will permit civilian agencies to respond to unanticipated contingencies. By design, traditional CIDA assistance is long term and inflexible, whereas military aid tends to be fast but one-dimensional. The Crisis Pool seeks to fill this lacuna by providing a new window on which both CIDA and DFAIT can bid (with the Ministry of Finance signing off on all activities). Likewise, the GPSF provides DFAIT with a highly flexible window, under the supervision of START and funded at the level of C$100 million a year for five years, to respond to a variety of conflict situations. In 2006, the main targets of the GPSF were to support engagement in Sudan (C$56), Afghanistan (C$14m), Palestinian territories (C$10m), and Haiti (C$5m), as well as Canada's contribution to global peace operations (C$8m).

Unlike in Great Britain or the Netherlands, however, Canada has not created any common pools to force "jointness" in the design and implementation of aid and other interventions. For the most part, each individual department continues to control its own funds, limiting incentives for cooperation on fragile states and post-conflict reconstruction. Indeed, most Canadian officials take the position that Canada has already been doing 3D collaboration for many years and that the creation of pooled funding may only create greater turf battles among agencies, instead of real, sustained incentives for greater analytical engagement to reach consensus about just where and how Canada should engage in fragile states.

Where to Engage? Warning and Prevention

A recurrent theme in consultations with Canadian officials is the need for Ottawa to be selective in deciding where to engage fragile states, given the real resource constraints on Canada's global presence. There is broad recognition that this choice will often be a political one, whereby the prime minister directs the relevant departments to jump-start a response to an emerging, high profile crisis. Indeed, the vast bulk of Canada's current engagement in fragile states is in Iraq, Afghanistan, Haiti, Sudan, and the Palestinian Territories, each of which is the subject of an interagency task force. To determine where else Canadian engagement might be warranted, the government has begun a DFAIT-led interagency process to identify fragile states, shepherded by the START Advisory Board. The idea is to come up with a list of twenty to twenty-five developing countries at risk of crisis, based on a common analytical framework. These countries will then be run through a decision matrix, to determine whether Canada's interests and values are engaged in the country, whether Canada has assets or capabilities to make a difference in the country in question, and whether this engagement can occur in a manner that minimizes risk to the Canadian people. The goal of this exercise is to identify perhaps six countries (in addition to the current high profile countries) that might warrant greater Canadian attention.

According to officials, this effort has been hindered by the fact that the main agencies—DND, DFAIT, and CIDA—continue to compile their own, varying lists of countries of interest and find it difficult reconcile their competing objectives and motivations for intervening. Once countries are identified, the next challenge will be to determine how to engage. As of late 2006, the relationship between the prioritization process and actual policy responses remained uncertain.

While Canadian officials and policy documents underline the importance of conflict prevention, practical policy advancements toward this goal remain weak. START has established a Conflict Prevention Division of roughly sixteen officers who cover risk assessment and early warning. START is also working to develop a Canadian mediation capacity. The IPS mandates six regional conflict issues groups co-chaired by START and the regional bureaus of the foreign ministry. These groups compile a list of possible countries to consider and they send these to the cabinet secretaries for approval. CIDA, meanwhile, is trying to mainstream conflict prevention into its work. Like many of the other donor governments, Canada continues to struggle to strike the right balance between initiating responses for post-conflict reconstruction and for conflict prevention.

Pilot Project: Haiti

One of Ottawa's most ambitious efforts to foster an integrated approach to fragile states has been Canada's heavy involvement in helping to promote security, good governance, and development in Haiti, particularly since the departure of President Jean-Bertrand Aristide in 2004. Canada's decision to play a leadership role in the international intervention there was motivated by multiple factors, including a sense of hemispheric solidarity and a desire to help alleviate poverty in the poorest country in the Americas; a long history of involvement in multidimensional peace operations; fears that the collapsed state was a growing source of drug trafficking and transnational crime; the influence of Canada's considerable Haitian diaspora; and Canada's longstanding diplomatic ties with the island.

Canadian agencies have generally recognized the need for cross-departmental collaboration to help build accountable public institutions in Haiti that might address the interconnected challenges of law and order, basic needs, and good governance. Given the limits of Canada's own resources, Canadian officials have sought to coordinate their own assistance and policy interventions closely with other donors through the Interim Cooperation Framework (ICF) linking the donor community and Haitian authorities. At a national level, Canada has created an interdepartmental steering group involving DFAIT, CIDA, DND, PSEP, and PCO. This group has supervised a number of critical cabinet decisions, including the dispatch of 100 civilian police officers to MINUSTAH under the CPA arrangement, the deployment of 106 short-term observers to Haitian elections, and the implementation of development assistance worth C$180 million for 2004-2006. In addition, START has collaborated with CIDA on a program to advance security sector reform in the country, based on a joint needs assessment.

Despite these successes, Canada's engagement in Haiti continues to fall short of a truly joined-up approach. Part of the problem is analytical. Rather than undertaking a joint analysis that might provide a unitary, or at least common, perspective of the country situation, DFAIT, DND, and CIDA have continued to generate independent political, security, and economic analyses, making it difficult for officials to see the interconnections between these realms and achieve a common situational awareness. This analytical disconnect has had real consequences for Canada's engagement in Haiti. DFAIT and DND complain, for instance, that the Country Development Programming Framework (CDPF) drafted by CIDA does not consider the drivers of instability and conflict within the country, nor discuss how Canadian development assistance might exacerbate or mitigate these underlying dynamics.

The fact that each of the "3Ds" maintains an independent reporting chain to its home department tends to reinforce these narrow institutional mind-sets, rather than revealing the inherent interconnections between security, governance, and development. This raises the risk that Canadian policy in Haiti will be shaped more by the institutional interests and mandates of various departments than by a comprehensive assessment of the dynamics on the ground, as well as an understanding of local priorities.

Conclusion

Canada's numerous policy statements and initiatives have encouraged more integrated approaches to fragile states. The principles set forth in the International Policy Statement, the creation of a relatively successful standing interagency task force designed to tackle conflict prevention and reconstruction in addition to humanitarian disasters, and the practical application of government-wide approaches in fragile states such as Afghanistan and Haiti, are all steps in the right direction. Despite its relatively good working relationships, however, government ministries continue to have difficulty reconciling their competing motivations and objectives for working in fragile states. Agencies have not agreed on a common definition of state fragility or agreed on a strategy for engaging such states, and there are few incentives across government to conduct common country assessments. Going forward, the Canadian government will need to identify and promote greater incentives to ensure that government-wide strategies are increasingly adopted in practice.

Chapter Four

Australia

Overview

Along with Great Britain and Canada, Australia is a frontrunner among donor countries in beginning to devise whole of government policy statements and strategies toward weak and failing states. Australia's policy interest in the links between poverty, poor governance, and violent conflict dates from the 1990s. However, its engagement with fragile states accelerated markedly after 9/11 and the Bali bombings of October 12, 2002, which persuaded many in Canberra that stalled development poses a growing threat to regional and international security.

Over the past several years, the Australian government has launched several initiatives of note. It has established a specific Fragile States Unit, housed in the Australian Agency for International Development (AusAID) but including representatives from other federal agencies, to strengthen understanding and policy responses to state fragility, particularly in the South Pacific. Separately, it has created a standing police force dedicated for deployment to overseas peace and stability operations. Finally, since July 2003, Australia has been leading one of the most innovative whole of government operations to date, the multilateral Regional Assistance Mission to Solomon Islands (RAMSI), which brings together the 3Ds (defense, development, and diplomacy) of the Australian government, as well as other key agencies such as the Australian Federal Police (AFP) and the Treasury, in an effort to assist the government of the Solomon Islands in improving stability, the rule of law, governance, and economic development.

Despite these advancements, Australia faces hurdles in translating its policy statements into agreed-upon doctrine and concrete action. It continues to struggle to come up with a unified concept of state fragility, and it lacks a government-wide fragile states strategy. Although the 2006 White Paper made a commitment to cross-departmental collaboration in Australian aid policy, the government has not yet instituted a process whereby such teams can meet to formulate common approaches to fragile states. Finally, there seems little support at the highest levels to either integrate the Fragile States Unit's analysis across government or to invest common financial resources in whole of government approaches.

Origins and Motivations

Unlike the United States, Australia's focus on weak and failing states antedates the global war on terrorism, being driven by the conditions in its immediate neighborhood, and particularly the so-called "arc of instability" to Australia's north, a region subject to chronic poverty and upheaval, where Australia has for many years been the most active donor and major military power. During the 1990s, the region's challenges, including in Papua New Guinea (PNG), the Solomon Islands, and East Timor, made Canberra sensitive to the potential links between poverty, conflict, and insecurity. The government's 1997 review of Australia's aid programs, *Better Aid for a Better Future*, highlighted good governance as a priority in bringing stability and development to the region.[87] That same year, Australia began participating in the Truce Monitoring Group in Bougainville, PNG. In 1998, Australia joined the International Peace Monitoring Group for the Solomon Islands. The following September, Australia deployed some 5,000 troops in leading the International Force for East Timor (INTERFET), a UN-mandated coalition that quelled the outburst of violence following the Timorese referendum on independence. Canberra played a lead role in supporting the follow-on UN transitional administration (UNTAET), which shepherded the province to independence in 2002. Australian involvement in East Timor involved a wide range of government agencies, engaged in governance, economic development, security, and rule of law activities, among others.

Australia's interest in stabilizing weak neighbors deepened markedly in the wake of 9/11 and the subsequent Bali bombings. These events reinforced the conviction in Canberra that precarious states can breed and enable a wide assortment of transboundary threats—including not only terrorism but also organized crime, weapons proliferation, infectious disease, and uncontrolled migration. Beyond being an obstacle to development and democracy, poor governance could endanger regional stability and bring new dangers to the shores of Australia itself.

In view of these trends, the challenge of fragile states became a core preoccupation of the country's development agency, foreign ministry, and department of defense. AusAID's 2002 report, *Approaches to Peace, Conflict and Development Policy*, underlined the relationship between poverty and instability, explicitly recognizing the role that development assistance could play in preventing and responding to violent conflict. In the same year, the Minister of Foreign Affairs and Trade called attention to the deleterious humanitarian and development effects of state failure in the Asia Pacific.

The government outlined a new approach to bolstering weak states in the region in its 2002 Ministerial Statement, *Australian Aid: Investing in Growth, Stability and Prosperity*, the product of consultation among all the main cabinet departments. The document specifically addressed the challenges fragile states pose to stability and security, including terrorism, HIV/AIDS, and the spread of social and economic instability and civil unrest.[88] It also acknowledged that the effectiveness of Australian engagement in such environments would depend on more integrated, joined-up work among its ministries. It established seven principles to guide Australian engagement in fragile states, including tailoring interventions to the specific circumstances of state fragility; ensuring no interruption in service delivery; engaging a broad spectrum of partner societies; strengthening the rule of law;

maintaining continual dialogue with the host government; harmonizing approaches with other donors; and addressing conflict dynamics where these are present.

Continued instability and insecurity in the Solomon Islands and PNG underscored the need for new approaches to help stabilize and reconstruct unstable and post-conflict environments.[89] This was matched by a feeling within government and relevant policy circles that traditional aid to the region was simply not working in poorly performing states.[90] In 2003, a Pacific Report of the Australian Senate identified state fragility as a leading threat to Australian interests in the region, arguing that working to prevent state decline was more cost effective than allowing states to deteriorate to the point where greater action might be required. Although the Department of Defense (DOD) remained hesitant to interfere in neighboring countries, fearing accusations of imperialism, it increasingly articulated the links between state failure, on the one hand, and transnational threats such as terrorism, on the other. Similarly, the Australian Federal Police, faced with more frequent requests to take part in stabilization operations throughout the South Pacific, embraced the challenge of fragile states as a core part of its mandate and recognized the need to work in a more integrated manner across government in such difficult environments.

In 2005, finally, AusAID released its own strategic approach to fragile states, arguing that Australia could not afford to disengage from such countries, without undermining the goals of poverty alleviation and good governance, as well as Australia's own security.[91] The development agency argued that aid could be effective even in poor performing countries, and that cutting such countries loose would only bring increased insecurity for their inhabitants and indeed the entire region.

Australia's 2006 White Paper on Australian Aid

The most comprehensive government-wide document articulating the links between security, stability, and development in the South Pacific is the 2006 White Paper, *Australian Aid: Promoting Growth and Stability*. Drafted after lengthy consultations among DFAT, the prime minister's office, the cabinet, AusAID, and the Treasury department, as well as input from Australian NGOs, the document emphasizes the need for Australia to use its development assistance to foster stable, functioning states.[92] To advance this aim, it calls on the Australian government to adopt integrated, whole of government strategies to address the root causes of corruption and to strengthen the capacity of countries in the region to handle transboundary threats. How this welcome rhetoric will be translated into actual programming remains to be seen.

Significantly, the White Paper focuses explicitly on development policy and assistance; it does not address the need for a whole of government approach to the entire range of Australian foreign policy and overseas aid. The goal is to promote unified country strategies and implementation frameworks covering all ODA-eligible activities, and provide a single, integrated framework for advancing development cooperation and combating state failure. Accordingly, the government has given AusAID a central role in leadership and coordination of this effort. The White Paper also calls for the creation of an Office of Development Effectiveness (ODE) to monitor performance of the overall aid program. While this is an important recommendation, the placement of the ODE within AusAID itself raises questions about whether it will have the independence required to provide unvarnished evaluations of the impact of Australian assistance.

United Concept of Fragility?

In practice, there is little agreement across government ministries about the utility of the concept of fragility or about its implications for the activities of relevant agencies. According to the broad definition contained in the 2006 White Paper, the category of "fragile state" encompasses "a wide variety of different circumstances, from post-conflict situations to protracted crises and stagnation, so assistance must be carefully calibrated to the individual country's circumstances and recognize the particular constraints of capacity and political will."[93]

AusAID is by far the most enthusiastic proponent of the fragile states agenda. Its concept has been shaped largely by discussions beginning in the late 1990s surrounding the ineffectiveness of traditional aid programs in many of its neighboring countries, such as Papua New Guinea, East Timor, and Fiji. In August 2005, AusAID created a small Fragile States Unit, which is housed at the development agency but includes individuals from other agencies, including the Department of Defense and the Federal Police.[94] Its role is to improve the Australian government's understanding, analysis, and responses to existing and possible future fragile states in the region. This is a good first start, but it does raise a question of whether a small six to ten person office within the development agency, with no programmatic resources of its own, will be sufficient to build understanding and appreciation of the challenge of state fragility across the Australian government. Moreover, AusAID itself, as an agency within DFAT, lacks the mandate, clout, expertise, and resources to carry forward the fragile states agenda and engage with such countries on its own.

Additionally, despite such momentum within the development agency, there is no commonly agreed understanding within Canberra of what "fragility" entails, about where and when Australia should intervene in such environments, or about how best to integrate Australian policy instruments to address the roots of instability. Nor is there agreement across agencies on the type of "effective" state the Australian government hopes to promote through its assistance. For AusAID, the primary objective remains reducing poverty and supporting institution building, including through a better understanding of how to create incentives for improved performance by weak and failing states. The DoD and DFAT, meanwhile, focus more on the potential links between state failure and transnational threats, such as terrorism and organized crime. The most recent two White Papers of the Defense Department, for example, highlight potential national security threats of spillovers from fragile states, such as from the Solomon Islands.[95] Likewise, the Federal Police has increasingly been engaged in stability and reconstruction efforts throughout the region, and sees its role in the fragile states agenda as pertaining more to security considerations. The ongoing Australian debate over how to define and approach state fragility was captured in a recent working paper by the Fragile States Unit, which highlighted the tensions and trade-offs in viewing such states through a national security versus development prism.

Policy Coherence

At the rhetorical level, all major Australian agencies strongly embrace the principle of joined-up approaches to fragile states. However, Australia has a long way to go to translate its policy coherence rhetoric into practice. This is especially true in terms of bringing the development and the security communities together in a more integrated manner, and expanding beyond policy coherence for development activities.

The government strongly endorsed joined-up approaches to foreign and development policy in the 2004 cabinet report, *Connecting Government: Whole of Government Responses to Australia's Priority Challenges.*[96] In May 2005, the prime minister released *Australian Aid: An Integrated Approach (13th Annual Statement to Parliament on Australia's Aid Program)*, which detailed the ways in which Australia is adopting new approaches to aid delivery, bringing together the development, foreign affairs, police, defense, and other arms of government to work on tsunami response, Solomon Islands, and Papua New Guinea.

Australia's Defense Department has increasingly articulated the need for integrated responses to national security concerns. In its 2005 National Security Strategy, the department stated, "Current threats to security require a whole-of-government approach… whether it is the whole-of-government response to terrorism, WMD, fisheries and resource protection, or in meeting the needs of neighboring states, the contribution of Defense is expected to go far beyond war-fighting."[97] Particularly in post-conflict environments, Australian defense officials call for more effective divisions of labor with civilian agencies.

The 2006 White Paper further builds on the need to better combat state fragility through interdepartmental cooperation, and especially in battling corruption and improving rule of law and justice. The document endorses greater interdepartmental collaboration in recipient countries, most notably through Australia's overseas development programs. As mentioned, this entails creating single country strategies covering all ODA-eligible activities, with AusAID playing a central leadership and coordinating role in this process. Whether this good first step will be advanced in the future to include whole of government strategies as they relate to all programmatic activities—not just toward development—is unclear. Still absent from this strategy, moreover, is any movement toward expanding the whole of government endorsement and common strategies to non-ODA activities, including vital security efforts of particular concern in fragile states.

Interdepartmental Coordination

Within the Australian government, there is no centralized location or committee that can endorse and enforce government-wide strategy toward fragile states. Interdepartmental coordination in Canberra primarily occurs through the creation of ad hoc interdepartmental committees (IDCs) on a country-specific basis to address particular crises, such as East Timor and the Solomon Islands. Accordingly, they tend to be more reactive than preventive in nature.

The level of involvement by the ministries varies according to the perceived priority a certain country has for Australia's international affairs policy. As such, they meet at various levels, from the Cabinet down to desk officers. For high priority cases, the Strategic Policy Coordination Group (SPCG)—made up of deputy secretaries from all relevant agencies and usually including the ministries of development, defense, foreign affairs, the treasury, and the police—coordinates and initiates such committees. The SPCG is supported by lower-level IDCs, where representatives from relevant department hash out specific issues.

Security policy at the highest level is coordinated by the National Security Committee of the Cabinet (NSC), which includes both ministers and department heads throughout the government and acts to integrate the views of government departments. It also meets on an ad hoc, as-necessary basis. While members of the NSC committee can provide policy recommendations and practice on whole of government initiatives, they do not discuss the issue of fragile states as such, and the Fragile States Unit does not have a space at the NSC. Further down the chain, foreign and development policy is made by the Department for Foreign Affairs and Trade (DFAT). When it comes to development, AusAID operates on a fairly autonomous level, implementing development aid and administering the bulk of official aid resources. It does not, however, have legal status to formulate official government policy, and reports to DFAT. On the security side, policy is made by the AFP, the DoD and the Australian Defense Forces.

All these departments work to coordinate their policy and actions through various IDCs, but the Fragile States Unit has no place at the table of the most influential high-level committees. Furthermore, a lack of leadership by the NSC on the fragile states agenda provides little motivation for other agencies to endorse and promote more sensitive programming and policy on state fragility.

Integrated Country Assessments, Strategic Plans, and Early Warning Systems

While Australia has issued several policy statements advocating for more integrated approaches toward fragile, failing and war-torn states, it lags behind other governments such as those of the United Kingdom and Canada in strategic planning and the creation of permanent units to deal with conflict prevention and post-conflict response. A notable gap in Australia's current efforts is the lack of fully institutionalized common country strategies that span both development and security concerns. Since 2003, the government has mandated that AusAID's country strategies take a whole of government approach, and the 2006 White Paper specifically calls for the institutionalization of such strategies for all recipients of Australian assistance. To date, however, such strategies have rarely been comprehensive, and many have been formulated in a purely informal manner. Furthermore, there has been little buy-in across relevant departments for truly integrated country strategies incorporating and balancing the priorities of the development, defense, and diplomatic communities.

Nor has the Australian government developed a standard

system to assess state fragility or to identify where and how Australia ought to engage. Currently, there are no government-wide indicators to measure state weakness and instability, let alone an early warning system to monitor and react to impending crisis. Australian agencies recognize this shortfall. In fact, the Department of Defense is currently pressing the Fragile States Unit to give more serious thought to devising early warning indicators that can highlight particular areas of state fragility. If this idea gets support, the hope would be to turn this into a major output for 2007.

Financial Incentives for Promoting Integrated Approaches

In addition to having varying motivations and objectives for engaging in fragile states, Australia currently has little money devoted specifically to programmatic activities aimed at fragile states. The small Fragile States Unit has a budget of roughly A\$1 million a year, funded by AusAID, which only covers personnel costs.

Unlike in the United Kingdom, there are no pooled funding mechanisms to encourage agencies to work together, and it appears that there is currently little appetite for creating such instruments. AusAID in particular has voiced concern that pooled funding could take money out of its ongoing desk activities. Moreover, there is concern that pooled funds specifically dedicated for fragile states would create a silo effect rather than truly encouraging greater integration within the Australian government.

As the other countries in this study suggest, common funding mechanisms are no guarantee of truly collaborative strategies and programmatic activities, since they may coexist with template driven or stove-piped efforts. Nevertheless, creating such a common resource pool could bring credibility to Australia's rhetorical commitment to whole of government strategies, by increasing incentives for different departments to work together in poorly performing countries—not just in development activities, but in all of Australia's programs. Similarly, Australia currently lacks a standing conflict response fund, forcing the government to draw on a modest annual budget that sets aside money for humanitarian and emergency work. In the view of several interviewees, this lack of a dedicated funding stream hinders rapid, joined-up interagency responses to fast-moving crises.

Post-Conflict Activities in Fragile States

While Australia is increasingly engaged in crisis response and post-conflict reconstruction activities, it currently has no standing unit dedicated to either conflict prevention or post-conflict peace-building, akin to the UK's PCRU, the United States' S/CRS, or Canada's START. As a partial solution to this gap, the Department of Defense is currently considering creating an standing inter-agency committee on peacebuilding and defense.

The International Deployment Group

Australia's main innovation in the post-conflict field lies in the creation of the International Deployment Group (IDG), a standing corps of over five hundred Australian Federal Police officers trained and made available for rapid deployment overseas for peacekeeping missions. Consistent with recommendations made in the 2000 UN Brahimi Report, which called on member states to establish national pools of officers, this Australian initiative is the first instance in which an OECD donor government has devoted substantial funds to create an institutional home where police officers can be mobilized and trained for deployment overseas to a range of missions of different scales, designs, durations, and objectives. Currently, the IDG's budget is A\$330 million, a figure expected to rise over the next several years.

Formed in 2004, the IDG is intended to contribute to regional stability and security in the South Pacific, by improving the delivery of physical safety, law and justice in target countries, including through capacity building programs. Prior to their missions, police officers take part in scenario-based, pre-deployment training at the IDG's International Training Complex. This includes a live-in program that replicates some of the hardships officers may face while on mission, as well as training in cultural awareness, remote first aid, search and rescue, and counterterrorism. This program is open not only to Australians but also to

Australia's South Pacific neighbors, including New Zealand, Fiji, Papua New Guinea, Samoa, and Vanuatu. Typically, officers serve between one and two years overseas, in operations such as the Regional Assistance Mission to Solomon Islands (RAMSI), described below.

Currently, the IDG provides forces to multinational operations in Cyprus, Jordan, Nauru, the Solomon Islands, Sudan, East Timor, and Vanuatu. To date, the IDG has been remarkably successful in delivering security and restoring the rule of law in countries where it is deployed. Based on this track record, the Australian government recently increased the IDG's funding, allowing it to support some seven hundred police officers. At the same time, the IDG has been less successful in providing and transferring knowledge in its capacity building efforts, and in incorporating its efforts into a comprehensive Australian peacebuilding strategy in countries such as the Solomon Islands.[98]

The Regional Assistance Mission to the Solomon Islands

Australia has developed arguably the most comprehensive whole of government strategy toward a fragile state of any donor to date, through leadership of the Regional Assistance Mission to the Solomon Islands (RAMSI). This effort was launched in 2003 in response to the conflict in the Solomon Islands, at the invitation of the government in Honiara. Blessed by the UN Security Council, RAMSI is a truly regional mission enacted through the Pacific Islands Forum. It involves representatives of some twelve states, including New Zealand, Fiji, and Papua New Guinea, although its staff and resources are overwhelmingly Australian. From the beginning, the Australian government has insisted that this civilian-led initiative—involving the deployment of civilian, police, and military personnel—reflect broad inter-departmental coordination among multiple Australian agencies and actors, including the prime minister and cabinet, foreign affairs and trade (DFAT), defense, AusAID, police, treasury, finance, and administration.

RAMSI is a police-led mission, reflecting the Australian government's conviction that inadequate law and order lies at the root of instability and conflict in the Solomon Islands. As influential observers like the Australian Strategic Policy Institute have noted, weak state institutions have left the Solomon Islands government unable to enforce legal order and provide justice, thereby exacerbating ethnic conflict. The government in Canberra, fearful that instability in its backyard could have deleterious security consequences in Australia, agreed to tackle law and order as one of its primary goals.

Australia has committed roughly A$200 million a year to RAMSI from 2004 to 2009. RAMSI's ambitious mandate is threefold: first, to stop the conflict; second, to restore law and order; and third, to promote sustainable governance and economic management. The wide-ranging mission has addressed everything from halting widespread conflict in 2003 to disarming former combatants, restoring fiscal and financial stability, and fostering social and economic development. These phases of stabilization, reconstruction, and development are not purely sequential, but rather overlap temporally and spatially. RAMSI has excelled in restoring law and order throughout the country. It prides itself in halting the conflict and disarming former combatants without a single shot being fired. It has also made a good start in advancing rebuilding in the country, by revamping the country's public sector and promoting good governance.

RAMSI's activities are coordinated through two primary mechanisms: the RAMSI IDC in Canberra and the Special Coordinator for RAMSI in the field. The Special Coordinator, a DFAT official, is charged with overall authority of the mission in country. His office acts as the central vein for decisionmaking in the field and reporting to headquarters. At the same time, the Special Coordinator has no direct control over the budget of RAMSI; the Department of Defense, the police and AusAID control the finances in the mission, with AusAID responsible for disbursing roughly half of the yearly A$200 million for development purposes, but also to programs in other agencies such as treasury and foreign affairs. This disbursement pattern has led to occasional disagreements and frustrations among agencies over how and where the financial resources can be spent, a result of differing objectives and a lack of a common understanding across agencies about priority tasks.

While the Office of the Special Coordinator lacks control over the budget, it has succeeded in bringing together heads of each element of RAMSI—including the defense, police, treasury, and development agencies—to promote broad coherence and consistency in Australia's activities in the Solomon Islands. The Special Coordinator heads the Principals Group, which includes high-level field representatives from different agencies. It is charged with hammering out common agreement on the RAMSI mission, and with communicating that consensus to Canberra. The RAMSI IDC updates the Australian government on its progress during weekly video conferences that include senior level officials in the field and in the capital. In those rare instances where Special Coordinator fails to get the police, civilian, and military components on the same page, issues for decision are transferred to a senior committee in Canberra. Every six months, the NSC meets to review RAMSI, and the SPCG meets more frequently as needed.

While usually successful, the coordination structure implemented in RAMSI might be a case of good intentions causing some distinct problems. There have been some grumblings that the lines of reporting among different arms of RAMSI, both in Australia as well as in Solomon Islands, are too confusing, generating tensions among different agencies working with RAMSI. Essentially, reporting requirements lead to at least three different lines of (sometimes overlapping) communication, which may be unnecessarily burdensome. On the other hand, this strategy has been effective in communicating information about the situation in the Solomon Islands as it relates to overall whole of government strategies, while allowing departments to maintain distinct control over their activities.

Another, perhaps larger, problem is the uneven input of the government of the Solomon Islands in shaping the priorities, participating in planning, and coordinating the activities of the regional assistance mission. Some officials on both sides believe that true coordination between RAMSI and the host government is lacking, and that while integrated planning and operations are welcome, there remains an imbalance between the pursuit of security objectives and long-term capacity building and development needs.

Many in Canberra and indeed around the world look to RAMSI as a model for peacebuilding missions that adequately incorporate the interests and capacities of development, defense, police, treasury, and foreign ministries. Nevertheless, RAMSI has experienced recent hiccups as it moves away from its immediate goals of halting conflict and toward the long-term, exceedingly difficult task of state-building—including instilling institutions and practices of good governance in the Solomon Islands. In the spring of 2006, a new wave of violence erupted. There are growing complaints too that RAMSI has not done enough to engage with or transfer skills and knowledge to the people of Solomon Islands. Continued volatility has made it ever more crucial for RAMSI to speed up its performance evaluation of the mission. This evaluation framework, established in 2005 and now led by DFAT and managed by AusAID, has been slow to get off the ground. It is hoped that the evaluation, which has developed performance indicators and benchmarks for success, will be strengthened and utilized more regularly going forward.

Conclusion

Interagency coordination in Canberra is strong, from high-level ministers down to desk officers, and whole of government approaches in foreign and aid policy have been explicitly endorsed across the Australian government. Nevertheless, Australia faces important decisions about whether to deepen its engagement with the fragile states agenda. On the one hand, it has created a Fragile States Unit at AusAID and embraced common country strategies in the formulation of development aid. It has also created the first ever permanent, deployable police force, as well as pioneered the most successful whole of government peacebuilding mission (RAMSI) within the donor community. On the other hand, Australia struggles to translate its many policy statements into real action. There is little impetus to come up with a unified concept and response to state fragility that spans both development and security concerns. Going forward, Canberra should push the Fragile States Unit to come up with indicators to identify and measure state fragility, and such measures should be incorporated into IDCs and into common country plans. Finally, Australia should move to include non-ODA programs into its whole of government country strategies.

Chapter Five

France

Overview

France lags behind many OECD countries in developing a coherent strategy toward fragile states. It has not internalized the concept of state fragility, much less adopted a whole of government approach to bolstering weak states or reconstructing war-torn countries. Individual ministries coordinate only intermittently with one another on the issues of conflict prevention and post-conflict stabilization, reconstruction, and peacebuilding. On balance, the French government has given more thought to the challenges of conflict prevention than of post-conflict operations. As in the United States, France's decisions about whether and when to engage weak and failing states in the developing world continue to be driven primarily by political and strategic considerations associated with a traditional view of the national interest, in contrast to donor nations like the Netherlands or Sweden that take a strongly neutral approach to their engagement. Similar to the US case, French foreign policy is strongly influenced by the executive branch, and the role of the president (Elysée Palace) should not be underestimated. Unlike in the case of the United States, however, considerations about the "global war on terrorism" have only marginal significance for French policy toward fragile states. In addition, and again distinct from the United States, France expresses a preference for multilateral action in crisis prevention and response, advocating a distinctive European Union approach to these challenges, looking to act through the United Nations where possible, and supporting greater capacity for the African Union as a regional organization.

Unified Concept of Fragility?

Despite co-chairing the OECD/DAC work stream on whole of government approaches to fragile states, the French government has not yet embraced the concept of state "fragility," nor has it developed an integrated, cross-ministerial approach to engaging poorly performing, unstable states in the developing world. This reticence has several roots. At an analytical level, French officials interviewed for this study suggest that the category of state fragility has limited utility, since individual countries (e.g., Cameroon) might shift among fragile and non-fragile categories rather quickly. At a practical level, they note, France is already engaged with many of the world's so-called fragile states (particularly in Africa) through its *Zone de Solidarité Prioritaire* (ZSP)—fifty-four countries and overseas territories designated as France's principal development partners. From this perspective, France is already trying to reinforce structures of legitimate governance and other institutional capacities, in a "common sense" manner. French officials also express concern about the potential diplomatic and budgetary implications of labeling aid recipients as "fragile," fearing that this could raise hackles from partner governments abroad, and create pressures within France to reallocate scarce aid resources away from countries that do not fit into this category but are nonetheless extremely needy from the perspective of poverty reduction, basic needs, and other development considerations. Finally, French officials stress that any decision to engage or intervene in any particular developing country will continue to depend on a political decision based on perceived national interests and the personal interest of senior French officials, particularly the president and the prime minister, "rather than on any category defined by aid officials or academics."

Notwithstanding this skepticism of the concept of fragility, French officials across government are beginning to recognize that agencies must do things differently—and do different things—in unstable or conflict-ridden environments. Similarly, they understand that development, political, and security elements of French (and broader donor) engagement should be better aligned and mutually reinforcing. Likewise, they are aware that the substance of French engagement will need to depend on whether the country in question primarily lacks the capacity or (as in the case of Zimbabwe) the "good will" needed to meet its obligations to its citizens.

Within France, the concept of fragility has won greatest adherence within the Agence Française de Développement (AFD), the country's development agency. AFD would like to see France adopt a government-wide fragile states strategy, but this is extremely unlikely in the near term. It is more likely that AFD will formulate its own fragile states strategy to guide its engagement in such countries.

AFD's ability to generate support for a French whole of government policy toward fragile states is complicated by the complex, fragmented nature of the French development aid system, which leaves it simply one of three (and by far the weakest) important players in this field. Under a regime established in 1998, joint responsibility for the strategic management of France's ODA is shared by the Ministère des Affaires Ètrangeres (MAE) and the Ministry of Economic Affairs, Finance, and Industry (MINEFI), whereas AFD serves as a principal operator in the field.

In terms of overall aid volume, AFD actually ranks third behind the two other big ministries. In 2004, MINEFI handled some 40 percent of French assistance, focusing primarily on macroeconomic and financial aid, including debt relief, contributions to international financial institutions, monetary and financial cooperation with the CFA franc zone countries, export financing, investment promotion, and the like. That same year, the MAE—and specifically the Direction Général de la Cooperation Internationale au Développement (DGCID)—was responsible for 29 percent of all French aid, which it tended to allocate, unsurprisingly, in accordance with diplomatic priorities. Indeed, while two-thirds of the DGCID's budget is devoted to ODA-eligible activities, less than one-third of DGCID's budget went to poverty reduction.[99] AFD, meanwhile, controlled only 10 percent of French ODA, which it directed to developing countries and to France's overseas departments and territories for economic and financial development that was designed to maintain social cohesion and to safeguard the environment.[100] Given this constellation of mandates, goals, and institutional cultures, policy coherence has remained illusory within the French development community—much less across the entire French government.

One moving piece of the French puzzle is the reorganization of the French development aid budget, which should empower AFD within the French bureaucracy. Although MAE has historically controlled a larger volume of foreign aid than AFD,[101] the government has committed itself to channeling a greater share of French development aid through AFD, and is in the midst of a transition that should be completed by the end of 2007. Even after this shift, however, the MAE will continue to manage aid related to broad sectors of governance and state-building (including support for political institutions and elections, public administration and finance, and policing and the rule of law), as well as providing overall policy guidance for the sector work undertaken by AFD (which focuses on issues like agriculture and rural development, health and basic education, environmental management, private sector development, job training, physical infrastructure, and urban development). This realignment of functions and funding may help clarify roles, and facilitate policy coherence and attention to international instability and governance issues.

AFD has begun to recognize the need to incorporate sensitivity to structural causes of conflict in its work, on the grounds that aid can ameliorate or exacerbate roots of conflict, but it is just beginning to put these ideas into practice. In contrast, the MAE and the Ministère de la Défense are less persuaded of the role of development cooperation in conflict prevention, on the grounds that violent conflict is rarely driven by poor economic performance (Cote d'Ivoire being held out as a case in point) and that development assistance is focused on long-term transformation rather than nimble crisis prevention.

Interdepartmental Coordination

There is no single focal point within the French foreign policy apparatus to coordinate strategy and planning for fragile states. The entity that comes closest to filling this function is the "African Cell" at the Elysée Palace, which formulates the main strategic outlines of French policy toward sub-Saharan Africa, the region where most of the fragile states that France engages are located. The cell includes representatives from the main ministries, including Foreign Affairs (both the diplomatic and development wings), MINEFI, and the Ministry of Defense.

When it comes to development assistance, interministerial coordination occurs through the Interministerial Committee for International Cooperation and Development (CICID). Following reforms in 2004-2005, the CICID is now charged with defining the objectives of French development policy; determining the countries targeted for assistance as members of the *Zone de Solidarité Prioritaire* (currently fifty-four nations); ensuring coherence of geographic and sector programs; and monitoring and evaluating the effectiveness of French aid policies and instruments. The CICID meets at the ministerial level only once a year, under the chairmanship of the prime minister, though more frequently (approximately once a month) at the working level.

Notwithstanding the CICID, an enduring obstacle to whole of government collaboration on fragile states is the strong tendency within the French government for ministries to remain vertically stove-piped rather than horizontally integrated. In contrast to most other governments, France has few real permanent structures of interministerial coordination, much less any common pooled funds. Accordingly, each ministry tends to adopt its own, rigid approach to particular challenges in crisis countries, concentrating on its own respective issue areas. The AFD, for example, focuses on traditional development, particularly sector work in areas like in education and health; the MAE, on issues of politics and governance, including parliamentary systems and the rule of law (justice and policing); and the MoD, on engagement with foreign militaries, including security sector reform.

With few human, financial, or institutional resources to

respond to failing states or help post-conflict countries recover, the recurrent pattern in France is to reinvent the wheel for each new contingency. Typically, the MAE will respond to a crisis by convening an interagency committee and creating a task force out of whole cloth. The MAE, MoD, and other relevant agencies then try to throw together a response, each using its own means (*"leurs propres moyens"*), often with minimal coordination with its partners. In the words of one official, *"Chaque fois on bricole."* ("Each time we cobble things together.")[102]

One obstacle to inter-ministerial coordination on weak and failing states is the lack of an authoritative entity at the heart of government that can direct independent-minded ministries, which jealously guard their prerogatives. The Secretariat General de la Defense Nationale (SGDN), which reports to the prime minister (rather than the president) comes closest to filling this function, being composed largely of detailees from other ministries, but it still falls far short of an NSC-like role in terms of its power to impose coordination. With the exception of a few areas (such as export controls) where it has been assigned a directive role, the SGDN is preoccupied with administrative coordination and information sharing, rather than direction and consolidation of government policy. Unable to "task" other ministries, it rather tries to persuade or cajole them to adopt a harmonized policy or a new approach, of use to the Elysée or the PM's office.

In the case of high-profile crises, the French government will assemble the Conseil de la Defense (Defense Council), which includes senior leadership from the MAE, the MoD, Ministry of the Interior, Ministry of Finance, and Chief of Staff of the Army. Because it is invoked only infrequently and meets at high a level, however, the council is an extremely heavy instrument to employ in crafting and implementing an integrated approach to preventing and responding to state failure.

Country Strategies

France's assistance strategies toward all developing countries, including fragile states, are driven by country strategy documents, *les Documents Cadres Partenariats* (DCPs).[103] Intended to provide a medium-term reference guide for all French official development cooperation activities within partner countries, these are prepared every three years (with a time horizon of five years) under the responsibility of the French ambassador, with input from the DGCID, MINEFI, and AFD. Following endorsement by the ambassador, DCPs are sent to the MAE before being reviewed and blessed by the CICID. The DCPs reflect an effort to shift French development policy toward the field, in order to improve alignment with local priorities, in-country harmonization with other donors, and coherence among French actors in the host country. As an experiment in decentralization, they are a welcome innovation in French development policy.

At the same time, they have certain limitations, particularly when it comes to fragile states. First, although they are intended to involve inputs from the recipient government and a wide range of private players in the host nation, in practice consultation and dialogue with partners is uneven. Moreover, while the five-year time horizon may be appropriate for countries in "normal" development circumstances, it is arguably too rigid a guideline for engagement with fragile states, which demand adaptability and flexibility to changing circumstances.

Beyond the time horizon, the DCP's limitation from a whole of government perspective is that it is driven by French ambassadors, who, given the traditional political and security focus of the French diplomatic corps, are "rarely *au courant* with the long-term development concerns," as one interviewee observed. This creates problems for the AFD, which must continually push for true development imperatives to be funded sufficiently, rather than being sacrificed for short-term national interest or security objectives. In addition, the DCPs are largely restricted to ODA-eligible activities, and accordingly, do not include critical security and rule of law needs in fragile states, including DDR, SSR, and rule of law interventions. French officials recognize the desirability of increased dialogue and input in policy formulation among the MAE, MoD, and AFD, so as to harmonize political, economic, and security considerations in creating a common strategy that could deal with the causes and dynamics of state fragility, but they are not optimistic that one will emerge.

Early Warning and Prevention

There is consensus across the government that France has adequate strategies and mechanisms for responding to "active crises," or *crises ouvertes*, which are typically managed by the *Centre Permanent de Coordination des Operations*, led by Defense. Where coherence and coordination are lacking and sorely needed is in the fields of conflict prevention and post-conflict reconstruction. In both domains, French officials recognize the need to begin breaking down vertical divisions among departments and to adopt a more horizontally integrated, concerted approach. Unfortunately, there is little agreement on the respective competencies of various ministries and the desirable divisions of labor such a whole of government approach would entail.

In summer 2006 the French government began exploring potential interagency tools to anticipate, and if possible prevent, crises in the developing world. This work is occurring in two separate locations within the French bureaucracy, described as "complementary" by French officials. The first is an effort by the *Secretariat General de la Defense National* (SGDN), a policy coordination arm of the prime minister's office, to develop a model for monitoring and early warning, with a time horizon of zero to two years, to anticipate whether a country is likely to fall into instability and conflict. (This predictive model would explicitly omit consideration of active conflicts such as Sudan/Darfur or Cote d'Ivoire, which are already the subject of extensive intelligence assessments and policy analysis). An interagency team has developed a draft list of countries at risk, approximately half of which are in Africa. The ultimate goal is to get all ministries to agree to a common set of countries of concern. This effort has been complicated by the very different lenses and time horizons that each actor brings to questions of instability and conflict. The biggest divergences have been between the AFD, which adopts a long- (or at least medium-) term focus on building the capacities of partner countries and meeting basic needs, and the MAE and the MoD, which focus on short-term implications of instability for France's immediate national security and foreign policy interests.

Simultaneously, the MAE has been exploring the creation of an intergovernmental crisis management unit, the *Centre d'Analyse et de Prévision*. Although physically located within the MAE, this would be a truly interministerial cell with a staff of twenty to twenty-five, designed to improve France's capacity to anticipate and manage a variety of crises, including both violent conflict and natural disasters. The unit would provide France with a standing rapid reaction capability to respond to crises in a timely manner, facilitating the sharing of information required for decision makers to take prompt action in rapidly evolving crises. It would also document, distill, and integrate lessons learned, so that France is not constantly reinventing the wheel in crisis environments. The proposal has met with resistance outside the MAE over the question of ministerial authority. Specifically, who will direct the activities of the cell, and will its members report to the MAE alone, or also to their home agency? Ministries are also reluctant to send high quality staff to the new unit and concerned about terms of reimbursement for secondments.[104]

The French government is united in the belief that conflict prevention should be a priority of diplomacy, but there remain significant obstacles to creating a standing interdepartmental unit that can reconcile the diverse perspectives, mandates, tools, and time frames of the various actors. Moreover, geographic directorates at the MAE are so caught up in the day-to-day that they find it difficult to focus on crisis prevention. Beyond these unresolved bureaucratic issues, French officials note the recurrent dilemma of moving from early warning to early preventive action. Given the dozens of NGOs that maintain indicators of instability and watch lists, information about emerging crises is rarely a problem, in contrast to political will. There is also the risk of official overload and paralysis, since the warning lists suggest that any one of a score of countries might be on the brink of crisis.[105]

In addition to the previously noted initiatives, in July 2004, the prime minister appointed Pierre-Andre Wiltzer, former minister for international cooperation and La Francophonie, as high representative for security and conflict prevention, under the authority of the MAE and in close cooperation with the Ministère de la Defense, with a mandate to think about how the French government might better engage with the international community in preventing and responding to conflicts. The clients for this effort include the Ministry of Foreign Affairs, the Ministry of Defense, and Ministry of the Economy. This *reflexion* (or study) has three objectives: first, to research how France might work with its partners to build the capacity of developing countries to maintain peace, particularly in support of the French-sponsored RECAMP (*Renforcement des Capacités Africaines de Maintien de la Paix*) initiative for Africa;[106] second, to explore possible French support for international initiatives on crisis prevention and post-conflict response; and third, to explore what can be done to build financial and human capacities of multilateral frameworks, including the EU, G-8, and Security Council, to respond to these challenges. Although an innovative initiative, Wiltzer's mission has faced severe and perhaps insurmountable obstacles to making any impact on French policy on conflict prevention and response. The office is tiny, including just four senior retired officials (two military and two civilian), and it has no budget, operational mandate, or directive authority over the ministries it is charged with advising. The mission is also something of a lame duck, since it will last only until Wiltzer himself retires. Given these limitations, the effort has struggled to gain buy-in from ministries that jealously guard their prerogatives and authority.

Post-Conflict Involvement

France is actively involved in ten or so post-conflict operations around the world, including in Afghanistan, Sudan, and Haiti. Rather than setting up a dedicated standing unit along the lines of the United States or the United Kingdom, however, France chooses instead to create new task forces and coordination groups on a case by case basis. The stated rationales for this orientation are that the menu of actions is likely to be different in each country (given unique historical and cultural circumstances), and that it would be diplomatically provocative to establish a standing unit to do contingency planning (seen as inherent in such standing units) prior to the actual eruption of a conflict.

Nevertheless, there is general agreement across the French government that France needs to become more nimble in post-conflict contexts, as well as overcome the severe capacity constraints on the civilian side of the government. AFD is currently carrying out a study of how French aid might be made more flexible in war-torn situations. There is also awareness that France lacks adequate analytical and technical expertise on the civilian side to engage fragile and crisis prone states. The MFA, for example, is charged with developing a French policy on post-conflict governance, but it has only three people in the entire ministry working on this topic.

Finally, there remains an important conceptual barrier to joined-up cooperation between civilian and political actors in post-conflict operations. The dominant French perception is that a hard and fast line exists between two phases of involvement: an initial one in which the main role will be played by the army in place to secure order and stability, and a subsequent one in which the military hands off control to civilian organizations to take on the traditional tasks of building local institutions and capacity. For the first phase, the military center in Lyon has developed a doctrine on civil-military cooperation, *Actions Civilo-Militaires*. There has been no similar move to develop a civil-military doctrine—or even a doctrine for civilian agencies alone—to cover the second phase of French involvement in such undertakings. One cost of this pattern has been an absence of institutional learning and a failure to create standing institutions to address the civilian dimensions of post-conflict operations. Likewise, there has been little effort to build up standing surge capabilities within civilian agencies to be deployed to crisis zones.

Funding for Fragile States

The French government possesses no common financing instrument for fragile states, conflict prevention, or post-conflict reconstruction that might create an incentive for interdepartmental coordination. Each ministry has its own budget and jealously guards its own priorities. During 2002-2003, there was an effort to win approval for a budget that would create a common pool to advance cooperation on post-conflict reconstruction, but it failed. A particularly problematic gap is the lack of any fast-disbursing window, outside humanitarian aid, to address emerging crises and post-conflict transitions in a flexible, adaptable manner. Funding for projects and programs in fragile states relies entirely on the regular budget cycle, submitted by ambassadors in October and cemented in January.

Another barrier to effective, well-resourced policies toward fragile states is the fragmentation of French aid policy. Unlike Great Britain, which has sought to reduce the number of its aid partners, France continues to spread itself too thin, operating in fifty-four ZSP countries.[107] Although AFD recognizes the need to be more selective, there are real political constraints on rupturing current aid relationships. Decisions about French assistance are made by the MAE and the PM's office, which are preoccupied less with the question of aid effectiveness than with France's Security Council membership, its bilateral treaty relations, its historical colonial ties, its diaspora connections, and its leadership of the Francophonie.

At the same time, the French government deserves credit for calling attention to the need for long-term engagement with fragile states, and the dangers of unpredictable fluctuations in foreign aid. As French officials point out, the donor community often suffers from an unhealthy "herd mentality," as donors stampede to respond to high profile crises, as in Sudan, providing an initial surge of resources but showing uncertain staying power, while ignoring other cases, like the Central African Republic. This huge disparity risks expanding the number of "aid orphans."

Conclusion

France's ambivalence toward the fragile states agenda is apparent. Despite co-chairing the DAC work stream on whole of government approaches toward fragile states, France lags behind many of its counterparts in terms of conceptualizing and defining fragile states, let alone creating institutional incentives that allow for greater collaboration across ministries. At least three gaps in

France's approach to fragile states will need to be filled if France decides it is serious about working more effectively in such environments. First, the French government should institutionalize new administrative and financial structures that encourage cross-ministerial cooperation and unity of effort. Second, Paris must commit itself to the creation of integrated country strategies that unite the interventions of all relevant departments (rather than merely development actors) in addressing the core problems of fragile states. The DCP model, as the foundation for France's assistance strategies with partner countries, should be expanded to permit greater engagement in areas like security and the rule of law. Third, France should continue work to develop a standing strategic analysis capability to anticipate and respond to instability and conflict, even as it deepens its post-conflict coordination mechanisms. The goal of these reforms should be to develop permanent institutional structures and instruments that will permit France to invest over the long term, rather than attempt short-term fixes, in fragile states.

Chapter Six

Germany

Overview

Germany's interest in preventing and responding to conflict and instability in the developing world antedates the US-led "global war on terrorism," dating from the experiences of the Balkans and Central Africa in the 1990s. The initial motivations for engaging weak and failing states were primarily humanitarian, focused on advancing human security and alleviating poverty in conflict prone countries. To improve Germany's capacity to respond to these challenges, in summer 2000, the Federal Security Council adopted an Action Plan for Civilian Crisis Prevention, Conflict Resolution, and Post-Conflict Peacebuilding. Since 9/11, these normative motivations for engaging fragile and conflict-prone states have been complemented by more sober national security considerations, based on the recognition that instability and violence in the developing world can have dangerous spillover effects for Germany and its European partners. Consistent with the multilateral thrust of German foreign policy, Berlin has framed its recent efforts in precarious states in the context of broader EU, UN, NATO and OECD initiatives on crisis prevention, peace operations, post-conflict peacebuilding, and development cooperation.

The principal governmental ministries involved in German engagement with fragile states are the Foreign Affairs Office (AA), the Federal Ministry for Economic Development and Cooperation (BMZ), and its implementing agency, German Technical

Cooperation (GTZ),[108] the Ministry of Defense (MoD), and—when it comes to policing and rule of law issues, the Ministry of the Interior (MoI). Germany's conflict prevention and peacebuilding strategy is focused on addressing and alleviating the root, or structural, causes of violent conflict. Crisis prevention is one of the five core themes of German development policy. By the same token, the German government considers poverty alleviation to be a critical dimension of peacebuilding. Certain innovations have cemented Germany's interest in fragile states—including the adoption in 2004 of an action plan on "Civilian Crisis Prevention, Conflict Resolution and Post-Conflict Peacebuilding," and informal principles of engagement for the BMZ for working in fragile states. However, Germany continues to lean heavily on the European Union in devising its own foreign policy goals and objectives, and it trails many other donors in terms of identifying and developing policy for a government-wide approach to working in difficult environments.

Towards a Fragile States Agenda?

The Federal Republic has not yet formulated a government-wide fragile states strategy, and the sector strategies that it has adopted to deal with matters of conflict, governance, and poverty reduction in developing countries tend to reflect the preoccupations of particular ministries, rather than any unified, coherent German approach that might exploit complementarity and reduce duplication. Additionally, Germany's response to the issues of state fragility has been slower than many of its European counterparts. Following the release of the EU's *European Security Strategy* (ESS) in October 2003, the Federal Republic expanded the Ministry of Defense's definition of security to include a more explicit attention to non-state threats. In addition, the Chancellor's office in spring 2004 commissioned an internal report about how the government could improve its performance in fragile states. The report proposed the creation of interministerial task forces and working groups, and even "conflict pools" along the British model. While there has been no follow-up to this proposal, it marked the first serious discussion about the need to create a government-wide set of objectives and goals for engaging in unstable countries.

Among the main ministries, the AA does not find much practical utility in the concept of "fragility," regarding it as overly theoretical. It prefers the more tangible concepts of conflict prevention and post-conflict reconstruction, activities that are heavily represented in the action plan on Civilian Crisis Prevention, Conflict Resolution and Post-Conflict Peace-Building. Like other European countries, Germany has not produced an official "national security strategy" document, instead deferring to the ESS, which identifies "failed states" as one of the five main threats confronting Europe.[109]

The Ministry of Defense, meanwhile, is increasingly preoccupied with weak and failing states as potential dangers to German and global security and as possible future locations for deployment of the Bundeswehr. In October 2006, the Ministry of Defense released its *White Paper on Security Policy and Reform of the Federal Army*. The first such document in twelve years, it explicitly emphasized the new threats posed by fragile and failing countries, while calling on Germany and its partners to adopt an integrated, comprehensive and multilateral approach to confront them. As the White Paper argues, "the chief determinants of future security policy development are not military, but social, economic, ecological and cultural conditions which can be influenced only through multinational cooperation."[110]

As in many donor governments, the concept of state fragility is most strongly embraced within Germany's development agency.[111] Since 2001, BMZ has expanded its reach to focus not only on poverty reduction, but also increasingly—though haphazardly—on programs related to conflict prevention and mitigation and state building.[112] At the same time, BMZ's quest for strategic coherence in German foreign assistance is constrained by its desire to be present in multiple countries at once. BMZ currently designates some seventy countries as "privileged" partners, and it finds it difficult for political reasons to ramp down its presence where results are poor, and concentrate its efforts on a more realistic number of aid recipients. The aid agency's internal bureaucratic structure also complicates policy coherence, since it divides responsibility for addressing conflict prevention and post-conflict peacebuilding, and development needs in fragile states into two separate divisions.[113] German aid agency officials increasingly recognize the need to build linkages between their two separate work streams on conflict and on fragility (a common challenge for donors).

The Federal Republic has made limited efforts to promote coherence across the German government in particular country circumstances. For instance, BMZ has cooperated with the MoD in Afghanistan, Bosnia-Herzegovina, Macedonia, and Kosovo. Likewise, the AA and BMZ have worked together on a seemingly successful pilot project targeting security sector reform in Indonesia. Building on these initiatives, BMZ in summer 2006 began to formulate a conceptual approach that could be a basis for a German fragile states policy. The resulting document, titled *Development-Oriented Transformation in Cases of Fragile Statehood and Bad Governance*, is designed to place Germany in a position to help poorly performing countries make the transition to sustainable development. BMZ has solicited broader buy-in from the AA and MoD—an effort complicated by its insistence that the focus of this fragile states strategy be on development cooperation, rather than address the broader array of German policy interests in such countries.

Evolving Instruments and Understandings

Although it lacks an explicit fragile states strategy, Germany's action plan on Civilian Crisis Prevention, Conflict Resolution and Post-Conflict Peace-Building has the potential—at least in principle—to address many challenges of fragile states.[114] Approved by the Cabinet on May 12, 2004, the Action Plan outlines 161 wide-ranging initiatives at the national and international level that the Federal Republic should undertake to help reduce prospects for—and respond to the outbreak and aftermath of—violent conflict. It requires the government to submit a document every two years detailing how it is implementing these recommenda-tions.[115] Implementation of the action plan is placed in the hands of an Inter-ministerial Steering Group, headed by an AA

Commissioner for Conflict Prevention,[116] charged with proposing and overseeing the development of cooperative mechanisms among the ministries to compensate for current weaknesses (rather than responding to specific crises). Its work to date has focused on four issues: security sector reform, joint financial instruments, refugee issues, and country pilot programs.

The main benefit of the action plan has been to mainstream the terms "conflict prevention" and "reconstruction" across the German government, and to endorse interdepartmental collaboration in managing the new security agenda. There is now recognition by domestic ministries, such as the Ministry of Justice, that they are part of a larger foreign policy enterprise, and need to increase their international capabilities (in this case, for rule of law programs).

Unfortunately, the action plan has severe limitations. It is not a plan, much less a strategy, but rather a long wish list of initiatives ranging from nonproliferation to democracy promotion to environmental protection, without any prioritization or road map to achieve them. Moreover, the plan lacks both the financial and human resources necessary to ensure its implementation, and a strong leadership structure capable of giving it political clout. Most interviewees regard the Steering Group as a disappointment, overly bureaucratic and unable to come up with real, prioritized, and actionable strategies to accomplish a mandate that is massive and unrealistic.[117] Although the legislation creating the action plan mandated that it be linked to the Federal Security Council (composed of key ministries) at the level of state secretary, the Steering Group has in practice been wholly detached from the top levels of government, and thus downgraded within the bureaucracies of relevant departments. This trend was reinforced by the advent of a more conservative German government under Angela Merkel in September 2005, which although endorsing the action plan is less preoccupied with creating a common, government-wide German policy to face the challenges of fragility and conflict prevention in the developing world.[118] The coalition agreement calls vaguely for the interministerial steering committee to be "strengthened," but makes no mention of resources.

Given the high aspirations behind the action plan, its results to date have been less than inspiring. The first biennial implementation report, approved by the German Cabinet in May 2006, revealed that many of the initiatives and structures conceived in the action plan had not been put into practice.[119] Nor, in the absence of resources specifically dedicated to achieving its goals, is there much hope for improvement in the future.

Obstacles to Joint Assessment and Integrated Country Strategies

A critical obstacle to an integrated and coherent approach to fragile states in Germany, both at the strategic and country specific level, is the *Ressortprinzip* (or "department principle") enshrined in the German constitution, which grants wide latitude to each ministry in formulating its policies and implementing cabinet decisions. This principle of ministerial independence (even sovereignty) means that the key departments—the AA, MoD, and BMZ—cannot be compelled to work together in confronting fragile states, or on virtually any other question, for that matter. Accordingly, except for extraordinary cases when the Chancellor provides guidance, Germany's engagement with any particular country tends to be fragmented, with the AA, BMZ, and MoD each pursuing independent courses of action that reflect their unique agenda and concerns, whether these be diplomatic, developmental, or defense-related. (Germany's pattern of coalition government exacerbates these dynamics, since it often places the relevant ministries in the hands of different parties). Although the AA occasionally directs the production of regional strategies, there is no standing government-wide process for assessing state fragility, drafting country strategies, and devising how various instruments of Germany's foreign aid should be allocated to fragile states, on the basis of German national priorities.[120] Nor is there any venue to force different ministries to work together to create policies based on a unified "German interest." Where disagreements arise, there are few ways to adjudicate other than going up to the cabinet level—itself a rare occurrence.

The Nigerian pilot project pursued under the action plan is illustrative. The motivation for this effort was to create a template for coherent German engagement, including a joint country analysis, to permit the FRG to respond quickly in the event of a brewing crisis. Headed by the regional director for West Africa, the process did not succeed in creating any sort of coherent government strategy; instead, the process resulted in a lowest common denominator wish list lacking either prioritization or an implementation strategy. Each ministry continued to look at Nigeria through its own lens, rather than forging consensus about the central challenges facing that country, and their implications for Germany. Whereas the BMZ stressed the requirements of poverty alleviation for the benefit of the Nigerian population, the Foreign Ministry and the MoD focused more narrowly on the diplomatic and security implications of potential failure in Nigeria for German national interests. The overall document that resulted was "not very encouraging," in the view of one participant, reflecting an undisciplined "shopping list." As another participant explained, the precondition for effective interministerial agreement is first to answer a fundamental question: "Are we as a government interest-driven or value-driven?" While such competing goals can often be reconciled in the long term, there may be short-term trade-offs. To date, German ministries have tended to avoid tackling this question head-on.

Germany's country strategies for development cooperation, typically of two to three years duration, are mostly worked out independently within the BMZ. Although BMZ submits to the AA lists of what it intends to spend money on in each country, its plans are already at an elaborate stage by this point, and the AA has neither the staff nor the capacity to evaluate or shift these aid allocations significantly, nor does it have a strong mandate to do so. Without significant changes made to create incentives for the different agencies to work together, it is unlikely that the FRG will generate coherent country strategies.

As might be expected, the German government also lacks a unified approach to monitoring and early warning. The AA maintains its own national interest-related watch lists, as does the MoD (from a military perspective). The BMZ monitors countries in crisis from the perspective of poverty and potential collapse, in terms of their impact on the inhabitants rather than German interests. It maintains a warning system that is unclassified but also unpublished. Across the German government, there is no standing mechanism to ensure that early warning triggers action.

In the absence of common country assessments and integrated strategies, inter-agency responses to the challenges of fragile states remain ad hoc and reactive, with the Federal Security Council or Federal Chancellery establishing country-specific coordination mechanisms to confront crises that threaten international peace and security.

Post-Conflict Activities

Germany's involvement in post-conflict stabilization and reconstruction efforts is a relatively recent phenomenon, and one that bears the imprint of the country's post-World War II caution in the exercise of military power. Nevertheless, Germany's global posture is beginning to change, as the German military transforms itself from a homeland force to more of an expeditionary force, though still at a modest level. German troops are today deployed to several global hot spots, including Afghanistan, Bosnia, Kosovo, Georgia, the Horn of Africa, the DRC, and (most recently) in Lebanon. For historical reasons, all decisions to deploy German troops abroad are inevitably controversial and require explicit parliamentary approval.

The German government has taken a distinctive approach to Provincial Reconstruction Teams (PRTs) in Afghanistan, instituting a strict separation between military and civilian components, with the civilian element serving as the focal point for interaction with local Afghan political figures and NGOs. The German model consists of a double-headed PRT, with a civilian side led by the AA and a military side led by a general of the Bundeswehr, each with its distinct chain of command and reporting structure to Berlin. The representatives of the BMZ and the Ministry of Interior—which manages the police program—also have separate reporting structures to Berlin. Although the model has been criticized by US officials for placing heavy national caveats on the use of military forces for coalition operations and for being overly risk averse, German officials laud their PRT as an antidote to what they regard as an overly militarized and coercive US approach to reconstruction and stabilization operations. They have also insisted that the PRT be conceived, and deployed, as an instrument to expand the role of the Afghan central government. Finally, they believe that individual PRTs should be multilateralized, so as not to appear dominated by any single nation.

Capacity for Civilian Crisis Response

In April 2002, the German government established the Center for International Peace Operations (ZIF), as a nonprofit entity financed by the AA. The mandate of ZIF is to enhance Germany's capacity for civilian crisis response, by recruiting and training civilian personnel for deployment to multinational peace support efforts under the auspices of the EU, UN, or OSCE, as well as election observers. ZIF is divided into three components: a training section, offering general courses on peacekeeping and more specialized ones on topics like DDR, rule of law, and mission administration; a recruiting section, which finds qualified applicants, manages pools of recruits, and nominates candidates for specific jobs; and an analysis section that provides case studies and modules for training, conducts independent analysis and gathers lessons learned, and seeks to fill information gaps for decision makers by providing them with quick summaries of policy issues.

In addition, in 1999, the German government joined with NGOs in establishing a Civil Peace Service (CPS), a consortium of experts in nonviolent conflict resolution, reconciliation, and peacebuilding who can be deployed around the world in crisis situations. In 2005, the CPS had a budget of 14.5 million euros to support forty-four experts in post-conflict operations, from the Great Lakes of Africa to Southeast Asia.[121]

Funding Instruments

Although the interministerial steering group for the action plan has explored the creation of common pools, it found little support for such funding instruments, and it is unlikely that any will be created in the near future. The German assessment is that the UK pool experience will not translate into Germany's constitutional setting, particularly the high degree of ministerial independence from the Chancellor's office. At the same time, interviewees expressed the view that "if you work by consensus, you don't need pools."

The Foreign Ministry has created a modest basket of funds, approximately €15-20 million a year, under the rubric "Support for International Measures for Conflict Prevention, Crisis Prevention, and Peacebuilding." This is a small amount but useful in terms of getting ministries to the table, and providing flexible seed money to initiate cooperation. One area where the AA has put these resources to good use is in a modest initiative for security sector reform in Indonesia, involving the ministries of foreign affairs, development, defense, and interior. The idea was to develop a joint strategy, provide resources for a common effort, and link elements of various ministries needed to accomplish the task. According to German officials, this limited experiment has worked quite well, primarily because modest funding (on the order of 1 million euros) was identified and allocated up front, encouraging cooperation between AA and BMZ, in particular. Germany has also devoted resources for strengthening the peacekeeping capabilities of ECOWAS, particularly through joint AA, BMZ, and MoD funding, and support for the Kofi Annan Peacekeeping Training Center in Ghana, as part of Germany's contribution to the G-8 Action Plan for Africa.

As in some other donor governments, there are tensions between the foreign ministry and the ministry of development cooperation on the allocation and uses of the latter's significant resources, which the former would frequently like to deploy for purposes more directly related to the narrow national interest. Experience suggests that where Germany is heavily involved, as in Afghanistan and the western Balkans, priorities among ministries are fairly well aligned. Elsewhere, however, the AA would prefer to see greater selectivity in BMZ's global engagement, including greater targeting of aid resources to German diplomatic priorities. Part of the coalition agreement for the Merkel government includes a commitment to reduce the number of BMZ's aid partners from more than seventy to a target of sixty, and AA has suggested some criteria to guide these decisions. Whether BMZ will accept these criteria remains to be seen.

Conclusion

Overall, Germany lags behind some other donors in conceptualizing—let alone devising—a fragile states policy. While BMZ has increasingly moved into conflict prevention, and the government has embraced more integrated post-conflict activities through its PRT, Germany has not yet succeeded in articulating a common strategic approach. Interdepartmental cooperation has not historically occurred, and it is unlikely that the departments of BMZ, AA, and Defense will cede authority to one another in the near future. In the absence of strong political guidance from the center capable of forcing different agencies to come together to reach common objectives, a unified German conception of, and implementation strategy for, fragile states is not likely to arise any time soon. Germany is likely to continue deferring to the ongoing work of the European Union and its European Security Strategy, in rationalizing how and where to engage in fragile states.

Chapter Seven

Sweden

Overview

More than any other donor reviewed in this study, Sweden treats development cooperation as the core of its foreign policy, and it has adopted an explicit whole of government approach to achieving the goals of "equitable and sustainable global development."[122] Sweden's Policy on Global Development (PGD) builds on a longstanding Swedish commitment to multilateral cooperation, including participation in UN peacekeeping, a pro-poor and rights-based approach to development, and a commitment to mediation and support for a "culture of prevention" (of violent conflict). More than most other donors, with the exception of other Nordic countries, Sweden's foreign and development policy is heavily framed in terms of advancing human security.

Since the end of the Cold War, Sweden has downsized the size of its armed forces and realigned its defense policy towards the mission of peacemaking. Sweden's policies on development cooperation, conflict prevention, and peacekeeping within the developing world are predicated on multilateral partnerships. As a rule, Sweden seeks to work through the European Union (EU) to formulate a more coherent EU-wide development policy framework, including common country strategies and harmonized aid instruments and mechanisms.

Although the Swedish government is aware that fragile states can become havens for terrorists and breeding grounds for other types of transnational security threats, its primary motivation for involvement in such countries is a sense of global solidarity. Indeed, Swedish officials consider US "war on terror" rhetoric to be counterproductive, and remain steadfast in promoting the centrality of sustainable development—for development's sake—in their country's foreign aid architecture. While interdepartmental cooperation works smoothly, the government has no explicit fragile states strategy either across government or within individual ministries. It also has done little strategic thinking about how to engage bilaterally in countries of concern and in countries that are not deemed "good performers."

Any Real Swedish Concept of State Fragility?

Despite its intellectual leadership in developing the concept of state fragility, particularly in the Ministry of Foreign Affairs (MFA),[123] Sweden does not have an explicit policy on fragile states, nor is there much impetus to create one. As an MFA study on the topic concluded, "The merits of developing a genuine strategy are limited in comparison to the downsides." Accordingly, "the focus of policy responses should instead be placed on how to develop and refine existing tools."[124] This is true even within the Swedish International Development Agency (Sida), where the general topic is covered by the policy department as an aid effectiveness issue. Swedish officials recognize the particular challenges posed by states with low capacity and/or poor governance, but they are content to align themselves with the OECD/DAC *Principles of Good International Engagement in Fragile States*,[125] and, from a security perspective, with the European Security Strategy, which identifies the challenge of "failed states" as one of five big threats confronting the EU. In addition, Sweden's defense bill mentions failed states as one of the main threats to Europe.[126] Beyond these general principles, Swedish officials emphasize the need to take a case-specific approach, given tremendous variation in developing country circumstances.

Additionally, Sweden does not have cooperation strategies with a number of fragile states where a host government is either lacking or where it is difficult to engage, such as Somalia or Zimbabwe. It does, however, maintain position papers and watching briefs on certain precarious states. Sida has also established a "countries in transition" category within its Africa Division, designed to encourage a transition to normalcy in countries where Sida does not have existing programs. On the other hand, the agency has only just begun to explore the links between security and development, including the potential of foreign aid to help prevent conflict and address the root causes of instability. Recognizing that 75 percent of its partner countries are affected by violent conflict, Sida understands the need to mainstream conflict sensitivity into its work, consistent with the vision of human security, including by promoting dialogue, physical security, and "structural stability."[127] It is unclear, however, how this insight will be translated into programmatic action.

More broadly, there is no overarching strategic concept governing Swedish engagement in fragile states. The Swedish government has strongly embraced a development paradigm as the core of its global engagement, but it has not yet engaged in frank discussion about how development efforts should be adapted to unstable and insecure environments. Nor has there been any explicit discussion of how development assistance in fragile states should relate to Sweden's wider foreign policy objectives. One obstacle to coherence, in this regard, is an ingrained Swedish reluctance to speak the language of national interests. As one official remarked, "Sweden does not have national strategic interests" (in the sense that the United States, the United Kingdom, or France do).

Perhaps inevitably, given these dynamics, the scope and nature of Swedish engagement with specific fragile states depends heavily on context. Swedish involvement in Afghanistan, for example, reflects a constellation of factors: the country's poverty, its production of drugs, and its status as a haven for terrorists. From a bureaucratic perspective, "it ticked every box." A similar grab-bag of considerations explains Sweden's relatively heavy presence in Liberia, perceived at once as a poor country, a source of regional instability, and an important arena for Sweden's EU partners.

In the absence of a guiding strategic vision, Sweden tends to lean heavily on EU policy and struggles to rationalize its own bilateral relationships with states in the developing world, beyond its adherence to the general goals of peace and stability. One illustration of this deference to Brussels is Sweden's reliance on EU-wide intelligence assessments, rather than developing its own national monitoring mechanisms and early warning techniques.

Coordination

The MFA is the focal point for interagency coordination on Sweden's international engagement. There is no NSC equivalent to set government-wide agendas and direct agencies, and decisions are taken on a consensus basis. Indeed, by Swedish tradition, the entire cabinet must approve significant governmental decisions—with the approval of at least five ministers (and disapproval of none) required to move forward on any policy. Interagency coordination occurs at four descending levels of government: at the ministerial, state secretary, policy director, and desk officer level. When agreement cannot be reached at the lowest levels, the matter is elevated up to the next level.

Nevertheless, interdepartmental coordination remains less of a struggle in Sweden than in many other OECD countries, thanks to a consensual political culture and regular communication among key institutions. The ministries appear to understand each others' roles and are pragmatic enough to involve relevant departments in discussions on matters of common interest. The modest size of the Ministry of Defense (MoD) further enhances prospects for civil-military cooperation. Given this natural collaborative tendency, the moderate size of the foreign affairs and defense departments, and the flexibility of existing interagency structures, Swedish government officials believe that there is no need to create new standing units to address conflict prevention, crisis response, or post-conflict operations.

Nevertheless, tensions do sometimes arise between the MFA and Sida on the use of aid to achieve political ends versus poverty alleviation. The Foreign Ministry is interested in political outcomes, particularly improvements in governance and reduction of corruption, whereas Sida tends to take a more input-driven, often technocratic approach, and is reluctant to recognize the fundamentally political nature of working in fragile states. Sida and the MFA also use different benchmarks to measure the impact of foreign aid, reflecting these distinct motivations. Nonetheless, the MFA generally respects the principle that aid should not be politicized once it has been granted to Sida.

Country Strategies: Sweden's Policy for Global Development

Although Sweden does not have a fragile states strategy, it is the first DAC donor to adopt and actively implement an avowedly whole of government approach to development cooperation in general. Coordination of interdepartmental policy begins with the *Joint Preparation Process*, required by law and aimed at creating policies agreed upon across ministries. The foundation for this approach is Sweden's groundbreaking *Policy on Global Development* (PGD). Passed by Parliament in 2003, the PGD establishes development cooperation as the central theme of Sweden's international engagement. It requires the state to harmonize the entire panoply of official instruments with which it engages each developing country. Policy coherence for development, in this sense, involves not only traditional development activities but also other policy areas like security, defense, trade, migration, finance, agriculture, environment, education, social welfare, public health, industry, and employment. The document opens the way for innovative experiments in joined-up government, including, among others, the MFA, MoD, MoJ, Sida, and parliament. The focal point for coordinating the PGD process is the PGD Secretariat, located within the Department for Development Cooperation of the MFA, which is charged with ensuring that every major government ministry contributes to the formulation of strategic goals in the government's global development bill.

Under this framework, the MFA takes the lead in shaping the overall foreign assistance budget and the specific cooperation strategies with partner countries, although the ultimate details of particular country strategies are often heavily influenced by Sida. Each bilateral cooperation strategy is intended to take the form of a single, comprehensive planning document, encompassing the entire range of Swedish assistance with that country. The sequence usually unfolds as follows: Once Parliament agrees to support development cooperation with a partner country, the PGD Secretariat in the MFA convenes an initial interdepartmental meeting intended, at least in principle, to bring any latent tensions to the fore, and to encourage agreement on a balanced, coherent approach and agreed divisions of roles and responsibilities. The MFA, in collaboration with Sida, then organizes a stakeholder meeting with outside actors to solicit their input for an initial draft cooperation strategy, drafted usually by Sida, and sometimes by the Foreign Ministry.[128]

The embassy country team then draws up a notional implementation plan in consultation with local officials and stakeholders, based on an assessment of development needs and priorities within the country. Sida and other ministries then prepare a more comprehensive strategy based on these assessments, defining a road map for how it is to be achieved. The development cooperation strategy is then submitted to government for its approval, by unanimous consensus, in a decision addressed to Sida. A development cooperation strategy is then approved. This short (typically ten-page) document is intended to guide Swedish engagement for the next two to three years. The contents of this strategy inform the annual letter of appropriation to Sida, which takes the form of a directive from the MFA.

Although Sweden has won deserved praise from the DAC for laying the foundations for a whole of government approach to development cooperation, translating the PGD blueprint into a truly integrated approach remains challenging in practice. The DAC has itself stated that "while the PGD mandate is clear and has high-level political support, much remains to be done to implement its policies and intentions, whether at headquarters or in the field."[129] On the positive side, the PGD has encouraged interdepartmental dialogue and understanding among the MFA, MoD, and Ministry of Justice on the challenges of fragile states, including the need to address issues straddling the realms of security and development, such as security sector reform. More negatively, true policy coherence tends to remain illusory. In many cases, the development cooperation strategies that result from the

PGD resemble Sida strategies, accompanied by little more than a description of what other Swedish actors are doing appended as an afterthought. In other cases, interviewees have complained, the Foreign Ministry has essentially set the content of the country strategy at an early stage, notwithstanding the commitment under the PGD to use initial meetings to solicit interdepartmental discussions and input. As a result, the collision of priorities among departments may not be solved, leading Sida, in particular, to try to insert its desiderata at the eleventh hour.

There are also shortcomings in trying to manage such a broad based development effort, with inputs from multiple actors, from a single line ministry. This organizational structure makes it difficult for other ministries to buy into the process and take ownership of PGD concepts. Establishing a body outside of any one ministry might be most effective in terms of bringing about genuine country strategies based on the various comparative advantages of each department, but it would take leadership from the highest levels to articulate how engagement in select countries is vital for global development and security and stability.

Funding Instruments and Aid Selectivity

Sweden has made no effort to create pooled funds to stimulate interdepartmental collaboration on fragile states. Nor are there significant, fast-disbursing windows that the MFA can draw upon to respond to help stabilize failing states, nurture fragile transitions, or fund critical post-conflict needs such as rule of law operations or security sector reform. Moreover, there are few real incentives to create such instruments. The Swedish political system establishes a clear distinction between governmental responsibility and departmental responsibility. Ministries receive guidance from the government once a year, along with their budget. Crises, however, can occur at any time, and the MFA is frequently frustrated by its inability to obtain flexible funds for critical purposes—such as promoting political reconciliation or security sector reform—since the vast majority of resources are already tied up in Sida's longer-term, programmatic work aimed specifically at poverty reduction.[130] To respond promptly in volatile and immediate post-conflict environments, Sweden needs to create a funding window for transitional assistance.

In addition to lacking pooled resources, Sweden continues to struggle in figuring out how and where to allocate its foreign aid around the globe. In the view of some Swedish officials, Sweden has not yet adapted its aid regime to the reality of today's conflict zones and fragile states. As a country, Sweden has made a vocal commitment to spending 1 percent of its GDP on foreign aid, on the grounds that the impact of Swedish aid is strongly correlated with its magnitude. There has been far less discussion about the types of activities Sweden is financing, and how to build effective institutions of governance, particularly in weak, conflict prone, and war-torn states, where traditional development approaches are not sufficient, and where the impact of aid on conflict dynamics may be either positive or negative.

Furthermore, Sweden continues to spread its aid too thinly and employ it less strategically than it might. Sida maintains large programs in some two dozen countries, with a total of sixty to seventy countries each receiving Swedish aid worth at least US$2 million.

In addition to spreading itself too thin, Sweden has found it difficult to work on activities in fragile states that are outside the traditional remit of Sida. While Sida has far greater resources than MoD or MFA for engaging in fragile states, the DAC criteria for ODA eligibility have limited its involvement in crucial areas like security sector reform. Beginning in 2006, Sida has obtained some relief in the use of its funds. ODA regulations now encompass the use of aid to support the reform of developing country defense ministries. Unfortunately, funding for other non-traditional activities including security sector reform and DDR remains limited, given MoD's scant budget and Sida's desire to ensure that its own spending meets ODA criteria, as well as Sweden's commitment to increase foreign aid to 1 percent of its GDP. Remaining limitations suggest that common pools may be a practical means of creating greater interdepartmental incentives for cooperation.

Civil-Military Coordination and Post-Conflict Activities

Sweden's armed forces are structured to participate heavily in crisis management tasks, including confidence building, conflict prevention, humanitarian action, peacekeeping, and peace enforcement. The entire defense budget for field operations is modest, however, amounting to $2 billion, or less than one-tenth of Sida's total budget. Sweden has also downsized its military forces dramatically in recent years, a factor that influences its strategies and global reach. Its current military plans are premised on increasing deployment of civilian crisis management teams.[131] At the European level, meanwhile, Sweden has been one of the drivers within the EU for developing a joint civil-military operational capacity, including integrated planning between civilians and the military. This initiative was approved by the EU in December 2005, under the rubric of "Effects-Based Approach to Operations."[132]

Sweden has been involved in several recent post-conflict peace support operations. Liberia is perhaps the best example of a Swedish whole of government response in a fragile state, given the involvement of the military, Sida, and a special envoy from the MFA. One of the main lessons of the Liberian experience has been that Sweden needs much better interministerial coordination to ensure greater alignment of planning, objectives, and resources, as well as between military resources and foreign aid instruments. Stimulated by MoD, the Swedish government has recently created a standing forum for civil-military coordination, chaired by the MFA.

Beyond Liberia, the leading example of Swedish cooperation among agencies in the field is in Afghanistan, particularly the Swedish-led PRT in Mazar-e-Sharif. In addition to its military component, the PRT includes a political advisor from the MFA, a development advisor from Sida, and an advisor from the Swedish police board. Swedish officials describe their PRT as patterned on the British model, intended to create a stable security environment so that reconstruction activities can be accomplished by civilian actors. The Swedish approach diverges from the American one, which officials in Stockholm characterized as consisting of a heavy military footprint, a blurring of military and civilian tasks, and a focus on unsustainable quick-impact projects. But it also differs, at the other extreme, from the German PRT model, characterized by heavy force protection, separate military and civilian chains of command, and a large civilian component that actually does reconstruction and development (as opposed to creating an enabling environment for other actors).

Sudan Pilot Project

Finally, Sweden has created an agency-wide approach to support conflict resolution, peacebuilding and economic recovery in Sudan, including the Comprehensive Peace Agreement reached in 2005. Officials in Stockholm describe the Sudan initiative as an effort to put the PGD principles into practice. Swedish policy is governed by the *Sudan Guidelines* approved in May 2004, after consultations between the MFA and the MoD, Sida, the Ministry of Justice, Swedish Armed Forces, and Swedish National Police. The guidelines establish the goal of Swedish policy as "to contribute to a long-term resolution of the conflict as well as to create the conditions for equitable and sustainable development."[133] Sweden's engagement focuses on four main areas: support for the peace process; advancement of human rights and democracy; provision of humanitarian and recovery assistance; and promotion of trade and economic cooperation. During 2005-2006, Swedish assistance to Sudan amounted to SEK833.4 million (approximately $125 million). In keeping with the multilateral thrust of the PGD, Sweden is also contributing to the Multi-Donor Trust Funds maintained by the UN and World Bank, and collaborating with the United Kingdom, Norway, Netherlands, and Denmark in the Joint Donor Team (JDT) in South Sudan.

Although the *Guidelines* are a useful beginning, conversations with officials involved suggest that there has been a fundamental lack of real discussion on overall, government-wide objectives and motivations for action in the country. Instead of resulting in an integrated plan that set real priorities and addressed trade-offs, the MFA-led drafting process was overly fragmented, with each agency advancing its own priorities and discussing what it could bring to the table in pursuit of these, rather than aiming for true coherence and complementarity of efforts. Humanitarian and development considerations tended to dominate issues of governance, security, and the rule of law.

In an effort to foster a more integrated policy, the government in August 2004 created an interagency working group on Sudan, under the Africa Department of the MFA, and in early 2006 appointed a special envoy for the Horn of Africa. While the working group has proved a useful venue for dialogue, it remains largely an information-sharing and consensus-building body, rather than a policy-making entity. The second main shortcoming of the working group is that it is limited to representatives of ministries. It thus excludes critical implementing agencies, including Sida, the most important Swedish actor working in Sudan. The experience underscores the limitations that Sweden's ministerial form of government poses for integrated approaches for fragile states.

Lastly, Sweden's practical ability to implement a whole of government approach on the ground in Sudan has been limited by at least three factors. The first is the country's tiny field presence in Sudan, including no more than a handful of officials in Khartoum and Southern Sudan. The second is the lack of integration between headquarters' efforts at policy coherence and those in the field. A third is the persistence of separate vertical reporting lines from the field to ministries and agencies, despite the close collaboration between MFA and Sida representatives in the field. In sum, there appears to be a strong disconnect between what appears to be a fairly coherent policy in Stockholm and practical realities and capacity limitations on the ground.

Conclusion

While Sweden is a role model in instilling whole of government approaches toward global development, it has no similar approach toward fragile states. Lacking specific national strategic interests other than promoting global development, Sweden is unlikely to create an explicit fragile states strategy in the near future. Instead, it will presumably continue to endorse and defer to principles that are made through the European Union, the OECD, or the United Nations.

Nevertheless, Sweden could improve its engagement with fragile states within the framework of the Policy on Global Development, by taking several steps. First, Sweden should launch a more robust conversation across government on the requirements for pursuing development in fragile states. The PGD has been fairly effective in mainstreaming development considerations across the Swedish government; it has been less successful in leading Sida to adapt its own ways of doing business in unstable environments, where new tools, methods, and partnerships are required. Second, and related, Sweden should ensure that the PGD process results in truly integrated cooperation strategies informed by a common needs assessment of each country. These plans should reflect not only traditional development considerations but also political analysis of the dynamics of fragility. Third, it should experiment with new pooled-funding mechanisms that are made available to a range of ministries and agencies, particularly for transitional needs. Lastly, Sweden needs to develop the tools and personnel resources required to ensure that the coherence mechanisms that it is creating at headquarters can make a tangible difference on the ground. Such innovations will require strong leadership from the highest levels of government.

Main Findings and Recommendations

As the country experiences analyzed in this study attest, the quest for coherence in donor policies toward fragile states remains a work in progress. The rhetorical commitment of many OECD governments to integrate their defense, diplomatic, development and other interventions in the world's weakest countries has outpaced practical steps in this direction. Notwithstanding a few promising innovations and pilot projects, individual donors continue to struggle in their efforts to define the purposes of policy coherence; to formulate a strategic vision to animate and guide their efforts; to create robust interdepartmental structures of coordination that assign leadership, clarify agency roles, and ensure accountability; to create new funding windows and aid streams tailored to the unique conditions of fragile states; to build the critical civilian capabilities required to address priority needs in post-conflict environments; to ensure the alignment and harmonization of their national efforts with local actors and other donors; and to evaluate the impact of their new strategies and policies. In other words, the whole is not yet as great as the sum of its parts. Below, we summarize these overall findings and offer recommendations to donors seeking to pursue joined-up policies toward conflict prone, failed, and war-torn states.

Conceptual and Strategic Issues

- **The concept of state "fragility" remains contested and controversial.** An effective whole of government approach depends at a minimum on a prior, common understanding of what a "fragile state" is. We find that line ministries often disagree on the definition and utility of the concept, on the countries to which the label should be applied, and on the question of which fragile states matter. Generally speaking, the concept is most popular among development ministries, which use it to describe a subset of poor countries where weak governance and state capacity are impediments to pro-poor growth.[134] Foreign and defense ministries tend to be more skeptical, finding the term a distraction from concrete challenges of crisis response and post-conflict reconstruction.[135] Foreign ministries are especially sensitive to the potential diplomatic fallout of publicly labeling particular states as "fragile."

- **Whole of government approaches may involve a wide range of agencies.** Notwithstanding the convenient shorthand of the "3Ds" (development, defense, and diplomacy), efforts to achieve policy coherence in fragile states often involve an array of other donor government departments, including ministries of finance, interior, justice, intelligence, trade, health, and others. Accordingly, donor governments must create coordination structures at headquarters and in the field, as well as training methods, which are flexible enough to accommodate this variable geometry.

- **Whole of government efforts fall along a spectrum.** Experience suggests that a whole of government ethos rarely emerges at once, but rather is the outcome of an iterative process. The gold standard, which is rare, implies that objectives, strategies, tools, and sequencing are basically agreed upon at an interagency level. At the other extreme is a situation in which the objectives are basically incompatible, there is little information flow among actors about who is doing what, and little knowledge of or interest in adopting an integrated approach. Faring slightly better are efforts to "de-conflict" approaches among departments so that they do not contradict or undermine one another, with at least a modicum of information-sharing. A more positive situation involves some harmonization and mutual reinforcement.

- **Whole of government approaches tend to work best as partnerships of equals.** Any coherent approach to fragile states will inevitably involve the pulling and hauling of ministries with different institutional mandates and priorities. Striking the right balance requires a structured process for assessing the sources of fragility, weighing the relative interests at stake, and determining how to sequence interventions. Such an outcome is less likely if there are gross asymmetries in the policy influence and resources of the relevant departments—as in the United States, where the massive resources of the Department of Defense cast a large shadow over policy, and where the national development agency lacks independence and is thus a beleaguered and marginal player. Nevertheless, experiences elsewhere[136] suggest that a balanced approach is still possible without an independent development ministry, provided that development considerations are taken seriously in crafting a national approach to fragile states. This implies, among other things, educating diplomats and other national security officials, who tend to be reactive and crisis-driven, about the need to adopt a longer-term time horizon and foster enduring structural change in troubled societies.

Policy Coherence in Fragile States is Great, but for What?

- **Integrated strategies for fragile states exist more in theory than in practice, and no single donor has formulated an explicit government-wide strategy for fragile states.** At a rhetorical level, donors acknowledge that policy coherence is essential to address the interdependent challenges of governance, security, and development in weak and failing states. In the place of a unified strategic vision, however, one generally encounters a welter of competing white papers and policy statements from relevant agencies. Since consensus rarely exists on the rationale and criteria for engaging fragile states, donor progress in developing new coordination mechanisms, innovative policy instruments, and common funding sources is highly variable.
- **Individual governments often avoid frank debate over the goals of coherence.** While all governments reviewed in this book regard fragile states as both a developmental and security challenge, donor capitals differ in the weight they give these two considerations. We find that donor governments

have begun to create new mechanisms, funds, and tools for interagency coordination, while skirting a prior, fundamental question about the purpose of this integration. Predictably, development agencies advocate policy coherence for development—that is, the alignment of national policy instruments to advance prospects for poverty alleviation and sustained growth in partner countries. (Sweden, which has made global development the centerpiece of its international engagement, falls strongly in this camp.) Foreign and defense ministries tend to be more preoccupied with achieving what might be termed policy coherence for national security, or the alignment of instruments to ensure that unstable developing countries do not pose a threat to the lives and well-being of rich world citizens. (The United States, certainly, is motivated overwhelmingly by the perceived lessons of 9/11 and the ensuing "global war on terrorism.")

- **The development community is deeply ambivalent about the whole of government agenda and the quest for coherence.** From the perspective of expediency, the growing national security salience of weak and failing states has benefits for garnering political attention and additional aid resources for fragile countries. Joined-up approaches also allow development ministries to leverage the contributions of defense and diplomatic actors to address critical aspects of state fragility such as security sector reform that may be outside the core competencies and legal authorities of traditional aid agencies. At the same time, integration carries potential risks for development agencies, which worry that their core agenda, including poverty alleviation and long-term institution building, will be subordinated to more immediate security and political imperatives.

- **The quest for coherence poses both intellectual and practical challenges.** In designing integrated approaches to fragile states, the donor community is essentially "flying blind." There is little accumulated knowledge about how best to combine development, governance, rule of law, security, and other interventions in fragile states, nor about how to sequence these components in response to specific local contexts. Such approaches carry high transaction costs and require laborious negotiations over how to balance the priorities and capabilities of individual agencies possessing very different mandates, priorities, organizational cultures, skill sets, and time frames, without homogenizing or losing the comparative advantages of the different entities. It is especially difficult to reconcile the desire for immediate results on the security front with medium- to long-term development programs geared toward structural transformation.

- **Achieving policy coherence in fragile states is a political rather than technical exercise.** This is true in at least two senses. First, it implies a political commitment on the part of external actors to support state-building, by bolstering the capacities of poorly performing states to deliver the political goods of legitimate governance, basic social welfare, economic growth, and physical security. Second, it implies a political process of dialogue and debate within donor governments, among individual departments and agencies, to define the country's general strategy toward fragile states, its aims in particular countries, and the best means to realize these goals.

Leadership and Coordination

- **A strong, authoritative coordinating entity at the heart of government can advance policy coherence.** Ambiguity over who is in charge of coordinating fragile states policy is a common impediment to joined-up approaches by donor governments. Where possible,[137] donors can overcome this problem by designating a robust focal point at the center of government, with clear leadership responsibility for drafting a fragile strategy, coordinating involvement in fragile, failing, and post-conflict states, and imposing discipline on independent-minded cabinet departments. Experience suggests that it is difficult to achieve such coordination by giving leadership to a single ministry—typically foreign affairs—rather than to a central, interagency coordination mechanism with firm directive authority, such as a national security council.

- **Standing interagency units have certain advantages.** Although most donors continue to rely on ad hoc task forces to address the problems of state failure and post-conflict recovery, some have created new functional units, staffed in part by details from relevant departments, to address post-conflict and (more rarely) preventive action issues. Such dedicated units obviate the need to reinvent the wheel in each contingency, increasing the prospect for rapid response and institutional learning. They can also help clarify mission leadership, as well as expose unspoken tensions, and force reconciliation of objectives. Seconded staff may also facilitate "reachback" to personnel and resources in their home agencies.

- **But such units are vulnerable to debilitating weaknesses.** Most importantly, they typically lack the bureaucratic heft and political backing of fully-fledged departments, which may jealously guard their prerogatives and fight a rearguard action to undermine their erstwhile coordinators. This is particularly true when new units are created out of whole cloth rather than built on existing bureaucratic structures or incorporated into established mechanisms of interagency coordination. Stand-alone units are also vulnerable to overreach, since their ambitions often outstrip their actual authorities and resources. Sticking to a realistic and well-defined mandate,[138] as well as assiduously pursuing buy-in from line ministries, is critical to success.

Mobilizing Resources

- **Donors have not faced up to the resource implications of this new strategic priority.** Our study points to a gap in the growing donor attention to weak and failing states, on the one hand, and current budget outlays and patterns, on the other. Resources to support integrated efforts in fragile states rarely rise above the pilot scale. This is particularly true when it comes to investment in critical civilian capabilities. The common mismatch between authorities and resources—when one agency possesses the former and another the latter—can cripple coordinated policy responses, whether by encouraging under-resourced agencies to try to poach resources from flush agencies, or leading well-funded agencies to pursue initiatives uninformed by whole of government principles. While some development ministries have large resources at their disposal for potential use in fragile states, these tend to be tied up in long-term programs, and thus are unavailable for prompt response.

- **Integrated funding mechanisms can encourage policy coherence.** Pooled funding and joint budget lines can provide a powerful incentive for collaboration, and capability for rapid response. The experience of the United Kingdom's Conflict Pools, in particular, shows that such instruments can bring relevant agencies to the table and encourage buy-in, lead to compromises on objectives, reduce time lags for addressing urgent needs, and facilitate the conducting of joint assessments and the formulation of genuinely integrated country strategies. Over time, they may play a socializing role among agencies, in helping participants understand the perspectives of their counterparts.

- **Pooled funds, however, cannot compensate for disagreement on ends.** Despite their potential benefits for policy coherence in fragile states, however, such pools have to date remained modest in scope. Even where pooled funds have been created, effective cooperation has often been stymied by the very different priorities of the agencies involved. There is an ongoing temptation to continue business as usual behind the window dressing of common funding, as ministries exploit the pools to advance their traditional programming.

- **Relaxing ODA eligibility criteria could remove an impediment to whole of government efforts.** The unique needs of fragile states require assistance that goes well beyond traditional development assistance, to include law enforcement and security sector reform in poorly governed states. For this reason, a number of OECD/DAC members have advocated relaxation of ODA eligibility criteria, both to accommodate a greater number of fragile states (many of which do not qualify for ODA based on the quality of their institutions and performance) and also to permit aid resources to be spent on nontraditional ODA activities.[139] An alternative solution would be for donors to make additional, non-ODA resources available, in the form of new budget lines. A handful of countries have moved in this direction, such as Canada (Global Peace and Security Fund) and the Netherlands (Stability Fund). But these are few in number and modest in size. At a minimum, donors need to make full use of the room for maneuver provided by current ODA definitions—something they often shy away from.

Coherence, Harmonization, Alignment, and Evaluation

- **Common country strategies remain the exception rather than the rule.** Rather than a comprehensive strategy, in most cases donor engagement with fragile states takes the form of parallel, largely independent diplomatic, security, aid, trade, and other initiatives. In current practice, such joined-up strategies are formulated only rarely and on an ad hoc basis, either in response to brewing crises (thus often too late), or as occasional pilot projects (as in the United Kingdom's Countries at Risk of Instability initiative). Even in these cases, the resulting "strategy" often takes the form of a lowest common denominator set of objectives, or of a vast wish list with little prioritization.

- **The quest for coherence can paradoxically complicate efforts to harmonize policy across donors.** While there may be sound reasons for donors to integrate internal strategies, instruments, and resources, doing so may reduce flexibility in engaging other donor governments, limiting the maneuvering room for individual ministries (of development, for instance) to operate with their counterparts in the donor community. This is particularly true when particular donor governments such as the United States and Sweden strike a very different balance among the security and development thrusts of their involvement in fragile countries. The US experience suggests that a commitment to joined-up government can deepen the tendency for unilateral approaches. This is true even in countries such as France, which places a rhetorical emphasis on acting through multilateral forums.

- **Whole of government efforts may also complicate efforts to align foreign assistance and other policies with the priorities of local stakeholders, including host governments and civil society.** With so much emphasis placed on creating coherence within donor governments, policy formulation and implementation may reflect top-down strategic direction from capitals, with limited (at best tactical) input from local partners. To counteract this dynamic, and to ensure the maximum host country ownership possible, donor governments will need to redouble their dialogues with host government and civil society actors, and provide real opportunities for local actors to influence aid policies.

- **Monitoring and evaluation pose additional challenges in fragile states.** The Achilles' heel of many aid interventions remains the unwillingness of the donor community to institute robust, independent, and transparent systems to monitor and evaluate the impact of their interventions. These evaluation challenges are magnified when engaging fragile states, given the variety of aid streams being delivered by different agencies, disagreement over the fundamental objectives of joined-up efforts, and lack of clarity and agreement about the metrics one should use to measure these overlapping (and sometimes competing) goals.

Assessment, Prevention, and Response

- **There has been far more talk than concrete action when it comes to prevention.** All donors play lip service to preventing the deterioration and collapse of states into violent conflict. But actual efforts to integrate the full panoply of policy instruments—or even to take an inventory of what those policy levers might be—have continued to lag. Nevertheless, the experience of several pilot projects— such as the UK experience in Yemen—suggest that the potential benefits of joined-up prevention efforts may outweigh the transaction costs involved.

- **Joint monitoring and early warning continue to meet resistance.** Few governments have created integrated monitoring and early warning systems to anticipate, and, where possible, to prevent state failure and conflict. Agencies often disagree over the nature and value of early warning, and differ notably in their views of relevant time horizons, with defense and diplomatic actors focusing on the short term, and development actors on the long term. Accordingly, different agencies tend to maintain separate watch lists and monitoring processes, tailored to their particular mandates.

- **Moving from early warning to early action remains problematic.** Even where robust early warning systems exist, the latter rarely ensure policy response. There are at least two reasons for this. First, donor countries are just beginning to build standing rapid reaction capabilities. Second, such alerts are rarely accompanied by concrete policy options, with associated costs, that could provide policymakers with a realistic set of alternatives among which to choose. Policymakers may thus perceive the choice as being a stark one of doing nothing or engaging in massive intervention. The lack of intermediate options reinforces the risk-averse instincts of most political leaders

Post-Conflict Efforts

- **Donors are just beginning to develop civilian-military doctrine, integrated planning, and joint training for post-conflict operations.** Painful experiences in Afghanistan, Iraq, and elsewhere have demonstrated the need for a joint doctrine specifying the evolving roles and responsibilities of military and civilian actors throughout the phases of external involvement. Such doctrine must reflect the fundamentally political nature of post-conflict stabilization, reconstruction, and peacebuilding. It must include provisions for timely contingency planning, beginning from the moment that intervention is contemplated, as well as detailed operational planning spanning all phases of the conflict. Since most civilian agencies lack a robust planning culture, militaries will need to export their planning capabilities to their civilian counterparts. While no "plan" is likely to survive intact once it confronts reality on the ground, the very act of joint planning—as well as regular training and exercises—is critical to facilitate mutual understanding, familiarity, and collaborative instincts between the military and civilian counterparts.

• **The donor community has been slow to create standing operational capacities on the civilian side.** Particularly for defense ministries, one of the biggest attractions of joined-up government is the promise of greater civilian capacities in the field, particularly when it comes to post-conflict environments, to free the military to pursue its primary mission. Nevertheless, donors continue to struggle to build up adequate technical capabilities within civilian agencies to design and implement essential activities in war-torn societies, as well as sufficient numbers of trained personnel who can be quickly deployed to the field in unstable environments. Areas where donors particularly continue to fall short include the realms of security sector reform and the rule of law.

Field Implications

• **Donor governments do not share a common vision of "jointness" in the field.** Donors have widely divergent perspectives on the roles of, and the appropriate balance between, civilian and military components of post-conflict reconstruction efforts, particularly in volatile settings. This is particularly evident in Afghanistan, where the different models of Provincial Reconstruction Teams (PRTs) provide a laboratory experiment in different national approaches.

- **Joined-up approaches need not imply equal implementing roles in the field.** The integrated formulation of country strategies need not require whole of government implementation, since the degree of involvement of any donor government's agencies will naturally depend on both context and mission. In the case of Haiti, for example, Canada's "whole of government" approach involves the Canadian International Development Agency, the Department of Foreign Affairs and International Trade, and the Royal Canadian Mounted Police (RCMP), but not the Ministry of National Defense.

- **Likewise, achieving coherence in the field may involve agencies of different donor governments.** Depending on the operating environment, the most practical means to achieve policy coherence may be to foster cooperation across donor governments, among different sorts of agencies—for instance between the development agency of one donor and the military (or diplomatic) representatives of another. This flexible variant of whole of government cooperation, which combines different components from different donors, is particularly attractive in volatile post-conflict contexts where security considerations complicate full spectrum field presence.

Recommendations

In view of these findings, we offer the following recommendations to donors, in the hopes of encouraging more effective whole of government approaches to fragile states.

- **Donor governments must commit to honest national dialogue about how to balance and prioritize the multiple goals and objectives involved in working in fragile states.** Aid agencies need to recognize that promoting development is not the primary mandate or mission of other government departments, which will be inclined to focus on policy coherence that advances the national interest. For their part, foreign and defense ministries should prioritize interventions that advance long-term institution building in fragile states.

- **A priority for each donor should be to develop a unified country strategy for each fragile state.** Such a strategy would set out the priority objectives for national policy and present policymakers with options (including associated costs). It would be based on a joint assessment of the root causes and current dynamics of instability and conflict; an analysis of the impact of state failure on the full panoply of donor interests; an inventory of the current strands of donor engagement in the country, and additional policy tools that might be brought to bear; and agreement on priority and sequencing of potential interventions, combined with a unified assistance strategy.

- **This common country strategy should drive a comprehensive assistance strategy.** The goal going forward should be to design a common assistance strategy that aligns and harmonizes, to the degree possible, the provision of security, governance, development, and other assistance. In some donor countries, multiyear development cooperation strategies continue to be designed in isolation, with only modest input from other parts of government. A truly integrated fragile states strategy would be more nimble and adaptive, capable of being updated as changing conditions warrant, based on strong input from unified country teams in host nations.[140]

- **High-level political commitment, guidance, and departmental leadership are imperative to advance this agenda within donor governments.** Even where agencies embrace the concept of fragility, there remains a strong bureaucratic tendency to pursue business as usual, for instance by repackaging existing programs and institutions under new labels. Given these institutional dynamics, senior political leaders must make a clear public commitment to whole of government strategies, and provide explicit guidance to relevant agencies about what is expected of them. In Great Britain, Prime Minister Tony Blair adopted such a tack, making cross-Whitehall collaboration a fundamental principle in engaging countries at risk of instability (as well as other global challenges). Departmental leadership is also critical. Experience suggests that resistance from senior ministers— whether driven by colliding priorities, turf wars, or personal animosity—will doom collaboration before it gets off the ground.

- **Professional incentives must be aligned to reward "jointness."** In most development, diplomatic, and defense ministries, participation in whole of government initiatives is often seen as a distraction from core institutional mandates and fast-track career trajectories. One way to overcome this natural resistance is to link professional advancement to "joint" service in central coordinating units and other ministries. More broadly, ministries can advance coordination through the creation of dedicated liaison offices, as well as the secondment and exchange of staff to other departments. An example of this is the creation of the Office of Military Affairs at USAID.

- **A starting point for policy coherence is an institutionalized, integrated system for early warning and assessment.** Experience suggests that prospects for success in joined-up approaches are much greater if donor governments commit to an integrated approach as far "upstream" as possible, through joint analysis and assessment of the roots and current dynamics of fragility in particular states. Such a rational, deliberative process increases the likelihood of arriving at a common diagnosis of the central problems, the stakes involved, and a desirable approach and division of labor in addressing them—in short, the essential components of a unified country strategy. It also helps to break down cultural and institutional barriers among departments, and forge unity behind a common effort. Unfortunately, there has been only modest movement within donor governments to create common assessment tools for use by multiple agencies, and to institutionalize a regular process of joint analysis. Notwithstanding promising experiments—such as the United Kingdom's Countries at Risk of Instability initiative—agencies continue to maintain competing assessment frameworks and methodologies, rather than embracing joint analysis as a matter of course.

- **Donor governments should consider devoting a greater share of foreign assistance to fragile states.** Recent donor practice has been to focus development aid resources disproportionately toward good performers, on the grounds that development assistance works best in good policy and institutional environments, whereas fragile states often face significant governance, corruption, and absorptive capacity hurdles. Recent evidence suggests, however, that carefully focused foreign assistance can encourage policy reform and institutional development in weak and failing states,[141] and that there is a wide disparity between aid to some fragile states and other low-income countries, despite similar governance and performance indicators.[142]

- **Access by agencies to pooled funding should be contingent upon genuine agreement on strategic priorities and joint oversight of implementation.** Central authorities must also place a fire wall (or "ring-fence") around these resources, which represent tempting targets for resource-strapped ministries, and are vulnerable to raiding.

- **In post-conflict contexts, there is no substitute for standing contingency funds that permit rapid crisis response.** One of the most cost effective expenditures donor governments can make is the creation of modest, fast-disbursing resource windows that can jump-start rapid conflict prevention or post-conflict reconstruction activities in crisis prone states. Such contingency funding is essential to avoid wasting precious time on preparing an additional appropriation of resources for the current crisis, or getting bogged down in the inevitable bureaucratic struggles involved in reallocating monies already dedicated to other purposes. As the US experience in particular shows, the lack of such a contingency fund is particularly debilitating to specialized interagency units, robbing them of the ability to respond quickly and establish their credibility across government departments.

- **Donor governments must develop new means to evaluate the impact of their interventions on state fragility.** Measuring aid effectiveness is never easy. There is a constant temptation to avoid honest assessments of outcomes, and to focus instead on (more easily measured) inputs and outputs. Monitoring and evaluation are even more complicated in the case of whole of government policies, since the desired outcomes are likely to be some amalgam of political, security, or development objectives. Getting governments to focus on the impact of their aid on the fragility of state institutions will be a constant struggle.

- **Governments must institutionalize new patterns of interagency dialogue that transcend mere information sharing, so that ministries consider the implications of joined up approaches for their current policies and programs in target countries, and adapt them accordingly.** For all the attention devoted to fragile or conflict prone states, the degree of national involvement and readiness to pursue whole of government approaches tends to reflect high-level political attention and decisions driven by classic national interest calculations, based on considerations such as strategic location, diplomatic implications, and economic consequences, as well as intangible variables like colonial history and diaspora linkages, rather than by careful analysis of cases, or technical measures of fragility.

- **The development of integrated fragile state policies within donor governments must not preclude harmonization of international efforts.** Bilateral efforts aimed at creating internal coherence toward fragile states should not neglect existing international efforts, nor result in increased cacophony in donor approaches to afflicted states. Donor governments should endeavor to harmonize their individual country strategies with other major players, and work with international arrangements already devoted to fragile and post-conflict states, for example through the UN Peacebuilding Commission.

- **The pursuit of whole of government approaches must**

be aligned with the priorities of local actors. Finally, donor interventions in fragile states are too often driven solely by the needs of external actors. As such, they are unlikely to address the problems that made these states fragile in the first place. To nurture effective, legitimate, and enduring institutions of governance, donors must support local ownership by aligning their efforts with the priorities of responsible, reformist elements of government and civil society.

Endnotes

1 Commission on Weak States and US National Security, *On the Brink: Weak States and US National Security*, Center for Global Development, Washington, DC: 2004.

2 United Kingdom Department for International Development, *Why We Need to Work More Effectively in Fragile States*, Poverty Reduction in Difficult Environments Team/ Aid Effectiveness Team Policy Division, DFID, 2005.

3 OECD/DAC, *Monitoring Resource Flows to Fragile States*, Fragile States Group, 2005, available at http://www.oecd.org/dataoecd/61/9/37035045.pdf; Stewart Patrick and Kaysie Brown, *Fragile States and US Foreign Assistance: Show Me the Money*, CGD Working Paper 96, Washington, DC: August 2006.

4 World Bank, *Engaging with Fragile States: An IEG Review of World Bank Support to Low-Income Countries Under Stress* (Washington, DC: World Bank, 2006). The World Bank's Fragile States Group title was formerly the Low Income Countries Under Stress (LICUS) unit. Lisa Chauvet and Paul Collier, "Development Effectiveness and Fragile States: Spillovers and Turnarounds," unpublished paper, Center for the Study of African Economies, Oxford University, January 2004, available at http://www.oecd.org/dataoecd/32/59/34255628.pdf.

5 Secretary-General's High Level Panel On Threats, Challenges and Change, *Our Common Future*, United Nations*: 2004;* Kofi Annan, *In Larger Freedom: Towards Development, Security, and Human Rights for All*, Report of the Secretary-General of the United Nations for Decision by Heads of State and Government in September 2005, United Nations: March 21, 2005.

6 Robert Picciotto, Charles Alao, Eka Ikpe, Martin Kimani, and Roger Slade, *Striking a New Balance: Donor Policy Coherence and Development Cooperation in Difficult Environments*, a background paper commissioned by the Learning and Advisory Process on Difficult Partnerships of the Development Assistance Committee of the OECD, London: IPI/Global Policy Project, December 30, 2004.

7 OECD/DAC, "Principles for Good International Engagement in Fragile States," DCD/2005/8/REV2. The Fragile States Group defines a "whole of government" approach as one in which a "government actively uses formal and/or informal networks across its different agencies within government to coordinate the design and implementation of the range of interventions that the government's

agencies are making, in order to increase the effectiveness of those interventions in achieving the desired objectives." Terms of Reference, Workstream on Whole of Government Approaches, OECD/DAC Fragile States Group, December 6, 2005.

8 The OECD/DAC commissioned the Netherlands Institute of International Relations (Clingendael) to coordinate this work stream, which examined the following donors, including experiences in the field: Australia (Solomon Islands); Belgium (Democratic Republic of the Congo [DRC]); Canada (Haiti); France (DRC); Netherlands (Sudan); Sweden (Sudan); United Kingdom (Yemen). The synthesis report of this effort was made available on the OECD/DAC web site in December 2006, at http://www.oecd.org/dataoecd/15/24/37826256.pdf.

9 Subsequent work may examine implementation of these evolving policies and strategies in the field.

10 DFID, *Work More Effectively*.

11 World Bank, *Engaging with Fragile States*.

12 USAID, *Fragile States Strategy*, Washington, DC: January 2000, archived at http://www.usaid.gov/policy/2005_fragile_states_strategy.pdf. USAID, "Measuring Fragility: Indicators and Methods for Rating State Performance," June 2006.

13 See http://globalpolicy.gmu.edu/pitf/.

14 Commission on Weak States and US National Security, *On the Brink*.

15 The 2006 Failed States Index can be accessed here: http://www.fundforpeace.org/programs/fsi/fsindex2006.php.

16 "The 2006 Country Indicators for Foreign Policy," *Canadian Foreign Policy Journal* 13, No. 1, 2006.

17 Ashraf Ghani et al., "Closing the Sovereignty Gap: An Approach to Statebuilding," Overseas Development Institute (London: 2005).

18 Susan Rice and Stewart Patrick, *Index of State Weakness in the Developing World*, Brookings-CGD Policy Brief (Spring 2007).

19 Commission for Africa, *Our Common Interest: Report of the Commission for Africa*, London: March 2005.

20 DFID, FCO and MoD, *The Causes of Conflict in Sub-Saharan Africa: Framework Document*, London: October 2001.

21 The document was an outcome of a strategic audit in 2003, which identified weak and failing states as one of three issue areas that could benefit from cross-Whitehall collaboration.

22 The CRI methodology held potential for cooperation across traditional departmental lines. In the field of security sector reform, for example, it would suggest moving away from simple "train and equip" policies toward the broader question of institutional development.

23 DFID, *Work More Effectively*. The document contends that fragile states have not received adequate or effective attention to date, thanks

to a variety of factors, including the current donor focus on good performers. In addition, aid is often delivered at wrong times or in ineffective ways (too much aid through uncoordinated projects). DFID distinguishes among four broad types of states: states with strong will and weak capacity; states with weak will and weak capacity; states with strong will and strong capacity; and states with weak will and strong capacity. See also Michael Anderson and Magüi Moreno Torres, *Fragile States: Defining Difficult Environments for Poverty Reduction*, London: DFID, 2004.

[24] DFID similarly resists efforts to categorize Iraq as a fragile state.

[25] Those working on fragility tend to adopt a very statist approach, asking what levers can be used to support fragile states and provide service delivery in difficult environments. Those working on conflict try to determine what is at root of the conflict.

[26] It will presumably identify priority countries where DFID must focus on considerations like governance or social exclusion. DFID already possesses important analytical tools, including the Strategic Conflict Assessment and the Drivers of Change methodology. The latter seeks to identify the structural and institutional factors (including political, economic, social, and cultural forces) likely to "drive" change in the medium term, and the underlying interests and incentives that affect the environment for reform.

[27] CIG, besides recruiting and deploying UK civilians (including police) for EU and other missions, also oversees policy and funding for peacekeeping operations. The unit is seeking to establish an on-call network of UK diplomats who have worked in conflict situations, including for possible deployment in future crises.

[28] Coordination takes place at three levels: in the formal cabinet committee structure; in meetings of senior officials (where more work gets done); and through the corralling function of the Cabinet Office.

[29] Like many defense ministries, the MoD takes a rigorous approach to assessment and planning. The FCO and other departments often respond that they do not have the staff or financial resources to conduct such assessments, and that the world does not unfold according to plan.

[30] In contrast, a genuine whole of government effort *can* challenge preconceptions of what ministries should be doing in target states. The CRI analysis of Bangladesh, for example, pointed to volatile dynamics, including the linkages among extremism, exclusion, and terrorism. In a setting with high male unemployment, one of the wellsprings of extremism, the analysis showed that it may be a mistake to focus primarily on girls' education, despite the conventional wisdom in the development literature, and the desire to advance that particular MDG.

[31] Bradford University et al., *Evaluation of the Conflict Prevention Pools*, London: DFID, March 2004, available at http://www.brad.ac.uk/acad/cics/publications/prevention.

[32] The UK experience in Sierra Leone helped inspire this decision. Clare Short, the minister for development, perceived violence in that country as a major obstacle to achieving development goals. DFID, MoD, and FCO, *The Africa Conflict Prevention Pool: An Information Document*, London: September 2004.

[33] For an internal evaluation, see FCO, DFID, and MoD, *Reducing Conflict in Africa: Progress and Challenges*, Africa Conflict Prevention Pool Performance Report, 2001-05 (May 18, 2005).

[34] In 2005, proposals exceeded the value of pool resources by 50 percent.

[35] Some strategies are only concepts, such as a general proposal to fund DDR in the Great Lakes region.

[36] DFID, FCO, and MoD, *The Global Conflict Prevention Pool: A Joint UK Government Approach to Reducing Conflict*, London: August 2003.

[37] In Sri Lanka, the global pool seems to have fostered collaboration on common objectives, in part because departments had no other resources, and were willing to cooperate.

[38] Divergent reporting systems have complicated integrated efforts. DFID has intense reporting systems; MoD has them but these tend to be input-based; and FCO does not have them at all.

[39] Dylan Hendrickson, "Donor Whole-of-Government Approaches in Fragile States: The Case of the UK in Yemen," prepared for the OECD-DAC Fragile States Group, December 19, 2006, p. 6. Available at http://www.ssronline.org/document_result.cfm?id=3015.

[40] Ibid.

[41] This effort has been complicated by the lack of a planning culture within the FCO. DFID is better positioned, since it has a culture of planning, albeit more focused on research and analysis and long-term institution building than on operational delivery in a short time frame. Moreover, the three departments have yet to develop common measures of effectiveness.

[42] In Basra, this has consisted of funding the team leader of the PRT and providing incremental support to people seconded to the PRT. In Afghanistan, it has involved supporting the ambassador's effort to coordinate UK policy in the field.

[43] Practical issues have also arisen concerning lines of authority, and command and control in the field.

[44] *National Security Strategy of the United States*, Washington, DC: 2002.

[45] USAID, *Foreign Aid in the National Interest: Promoting Freedom, Security and Opportunity*, 2003.

[46] USAID, *Fragile States Strategy*, Washington, DC: 2005.

[47] *National Security Strategy of the United States*, Washington, DC: 2006.

[48] *National Defense Strategy of the United States,* Washington, DC: 2005.

[49] Testimony of George Tenet to Senate Select Committee on Intelligence, "The World Wide Threat in 2003: Evolving Dangers in a Complex World," February 12, 2003.

[50] Stephen D. Krasner and Carlos Pascual, "Addressing State Failure," *Foreign Affairs* (July/August 2005).

[51] Secretary of State Condoleezza Rice, "Transformational Diplomacy," speech at Georgetown University, January 18, 2006, available at http://www.state.gov/secretary/rm/2006/59306.htm.

[52] USAID, *US Foreign Aid: Meeting the Challenge of the Twenty-First Century,* Washington, DC: 2004.

[53] Presidential Decision Directive 56, *The Clinton Administration's Policy on Managing Complex Contingency Operations,* May 1997.

[54] National Security Presidential Directive (NSPD)-44, *Management of Interagency Efforts Concerning Reconstruction and Stabilization,* December 7, 2005. Archived at http://www.fas.org/irp/offdocs/nspd/nspd-44.html.

[55] Ibid.

[56] One can contrast this with the ability of its Canadian counterpart—the Stabilization and Reconstruction Task Force (START)—to obtain a contingency fund of 100 million Canadian dollars, despite Canada's far smaller international involvement in such operations.

[57] *Defense Science Board 2004 Summer Study on Transition to and from Hostilities,* Office of the Undersecretary of Defense for Acquisitions, Technology and Logistics, Department of Defense, December 2004, available at http://www.acq.osd.mil/dsb/reports/2004-12-DSB_SS_Report_Final.pdf.

[58] Department of Defense Directive 3000.05, *Military Support for Stability, Security, Transition, and Reconstruction (SSTR) Operations,* November 28, 2005, available at http://www.dtic.mil/whs/directives/corres/html/300005.htm.

[59] Developing such a capability represents a huge cultural shift within the department, staffed by foreign service officers more adept at diplomatic reporting and analysis than running actual operations or programs.

[60] To further this objective, some experts have called on Congress to pass legislation akin to the landmark Goldwater-Nichols Department of Defense Reorganization Act of 1986, which, in addition to creating the Joint Chiefs of Staff, made "joint" service a precondition for career advancement. Clark A. Murdock and Michelle A. Flournoy, *Beyond Goldwater-Nichols: US Government and Defense Reform for a New Strategic Era, Phase 2 Report,* Washington, DC: Center for Strategic and International Studies, 2005.

[61] PRTs built on small civil affairs teams that had been deployed to assess humanitarian needs and coordinate with civilian actors. By

December 2006, there were some twenty-four PRTs spread throughout Afghanistan, all having come under ISAF command.

[62] Department of State, Office of the Coordinator for Reconstruction and Stabilization; Department of Defense, Joint Center for Operational Analysis/US Joint Forces Command; USAID, Bureau for Policy and Program Coordination, *Provincial Reconstruction Teams in Afghanistan: An Interagency Assessment*, June 2006, p. 10, available at http://pdf.usaid.gov/pdf_docs/PNADG252.pdf.

[63] Robert M. Perito, "The US Experience with Provincial Reconstruction Teams in Afghanistan: Lessons Identified," *USIP Special Report* 152, Washington, DC: October 2005.

[64] In addition, the "light footprint" approach has often led US PRTs to empower local warlords, notwithstanding their mandate to help expand the reach of the Afghan central government.

[65] *Provincial Reconstruction Teams in Afghanistan*, p. 10.

[66] Victoria Wheeler and Adele Harmer, eds., *Resetting the Rules of Engagement: Trends and Issues in Military-Humanitarian Relations*, Overseas Development Institute, HPG Report 21, London: March 2006.

[67] Krasner and Pascual, "Addressing State Failure."

[68] Secretary of State Condoleezza Rice, "Transformational Diplomacy," Washington, DC: January 2006.

[69] The category currently includes Afghanistan, Colombia, Haiti, Sudan, Liberia, Kosovo, Iraq, Democratic Republic of Congo, Nepal, Cote d'Ivoire, Sierra Leone, and Somalia.

[70] In July 2006, the DFA added a sixth category to cover "global or regional" issues.

[71] The Treasury Department, for example, controls US relations with international financial institutions, as well as the extension of debt relief, and the provision of technical assistance.

[72] Larry Nowels and Connie Veillette, *Restructuring US Foreign Aid: The Role of the Director of Foreign Assistance*, CRS Report for Congress, June 16, 2006. Funds appropriated to DoD for reconstruction and stabilization totaled $4.66 billion in FY06, plus another $500 million for the flexible Commanders' Emergency Response Program (CERP), in addition to $7 billion in the FY05 supplemental budget for training and equipping security forces in those countries.

[73] Miriam Pemberton and Lawrence Korb, *A Unified Security Budget for the United States*, Foreign Policy in Focus, Washington, DC: May 2006.

[74] Patrick and Brown, *Fragile States and US Foreign Assistance*.

[75] *Canada's International Policy Statement: A Role of Pride and Influence in the World*, April 9, 2005, available at http://www.itcan-cican.gc.ca/ips/menu-en.asp.

[76] United Nations, *A More Secure World: Our Shared Responsibility*, Report of the Secretary-General's High Level Panel on Threats, Challenges

and Change, 2004.

77 The Canadian government has supported the creation and publication of the *Human Security Report*, available at http://www.humansecurityreport.info.

78 OECD/DAC, *Conflict, Peace and Development Cooperation on the Threshold of the Twenty-First Century*, Paris: OECD, 1997.

79 *Canada's International Policy Statement*.

80 Democracy was a major theme of the "speech from the throne" that inaugurated the new government. In addition, the government has convened a new Democracy Council that brings together DFAIT and CIDA.

81 DFAIT wrote the overview of the IPS, and each agency wrote its own particular section. While there is some connective tissue linking the central pillars, there was less integration than hoped.

82 CIDA, *Guidelines for Effective Development Cooperation in Fragile States*, Gatineau, Quebec: November 2005.

83 The IPS envisions an increase in Canadian Forces by 5,000, in order to allow for greater overseas operations, along with an additional C$13 billion in funding.

84 While interagency collaboration runs comparatively smoothly, DND has remarked that cultural differences still remain an obstacle to interdepartmental cooperation in the field, particularly in violent circumstances.

85 *International Policy Statement*.

86 These countries include Bangladesh, Benin, Bolivia, Burkina Faso, Cambodia, Cameroon, Ethiopia, Ghana, Guyana, Honduras, Indonesia, Kenya, Malawi, Mali, Mozambique, Nicaragua, Niger, Pakistan, Rwanda, Senegal, Sri Lanka, Tanzania, Vietnam, Ukraine, and Zambia.

87 Australian Agency for International Development (AusAID), *Better Aid for a Better Future*, The Hon. Alexander Downer MP, minister for foreign affairs, Seventh Annual Report to Parliament on Australia's Development Cooperation Program and The Government's Response to the Committee of Review of Australia's Overseas Aid Program, Canberra: November 1997.

88 2002 Ministerial Statement, *Australian Aid: Investing in Growth, Stability and Prosperity*, September 2002.

89 Elsina Wainwright, *The Solomon Islands: Our Failing Neighbor* (Canberra: Australian Strategic Policy Institute, 2003).

90 Helen Hughes, "Aid Has Failed the Pacific," *Issue Analysis* no. 33 (7 May 2003).

91 Ian Anderson, *Fragile States: What Is International Experience Telling Us*, Canberra: AusAID, 2005.

92 White Paper on the Australian Government's Overseas Program, *Australian Aid: Promoting Growth and Stability*, Canberra: June 2006.

The White Paper's other main themes included accelerating economic growth, investing in people, and promoting regional stability and cooperation.

93 White Paper, 2006.

94 Glaringly absent in the Fragile States Unit are members of the Department of Foreign Affairs and Trade.

95 Department of Defense, *Australia's National Security: A Defense Update*, Canberra: 2003, 2005.

96 Australian Government, *Connecting Government: Whole of Government Responses to Australia's Priority Challenges*, Canberra: 2004.

97 Department of Defense, 2005.

98 Gordon Peake and Kaysie Studdard Brown, "Policebuilding: The International Deployment Group in the Solomon Islands," *International Peacekeeping* 12, no.4 (Winter 2005).

99 OECD, *DAC Peer Review: Main Findings and Recommendations, France* (2004), available at http://www.oecd.org/document/11/0,2340,fr_2649_34603_3207073 1_1_1_1_1,00.html, p. 56.

100 In 2004, MINEFI was responsible for some 40% of French aid; the MAE for 29%, and AFD only for 10%. The current division of responsibilities tends to make relations between MAE and AFD more competitive than complementary. OECD, *DAC Peer Review: France*, pp. 10, 14.

101 The MAE's role in French foreign aid reflects the 1999 decision to merge the Ministère des Affaires Étrangeres and the Ministère de la Cooperation et de La Francophonie, which had long been separate entities. This division lives on internally within the MAE, where there remains a deputy minister for Economic Cooperation and a director-general for International Development Cooperation (DGCID).

102 France does have a standing interagency mechanism to respond to humanitarian crises, *La Division de l'Accion Humanitaire*, though its mandate and resources are restricted.

103 OECD, *DAC Peer Review: France*.

104 The MoD has of course several early warning cells of its own, including the Direction des Affaires Strategiques, the Direction du Renseignement Militaire, and the Direction Générale de la Securité Éxterieure.

105 Wiltzer's office has proposed creating a Force Africain de Développement, cosponsored by the AU and EU, which would complement the AU's planned African Standby Force.

106 http://www.diplomatie.gouv.fr/fr/pays-zones-geo_833/afrique_1063/renforcement-capacites-africaines-maintien-paix-recamp_335/colonne-droite_2519/textes-reference_2520/renforcement-capacites-africaines-maintien-paix-

recamp_4429.html.

[107] OECD, *DAC Peer Review: France*, p. 12. AFD has gotten better in this regard, now avoiding aid commitments of less than 6 million euros, to avoid problems of proliferation and burdens on recipients. It also avoids soft loans less than 15 million euros. France has a pronounced tendency to prefer projects to programs.

[108] GTZ is a private government agency established in 1975 to manage and implement development projects using BMZ funds, as well as to offer technical services to other German ministries, the European Commission, World Bank, and UN agencies, among others.

[109] Council of the European Union, *A Secure Europe in a Better World – The European Security Strategy*, Brussels: December 12, 2003.

[110] Federal Ministry of Defense, *White Paper 2006 on German Security Policy and the Future of the Bundeswehr*, Berlin, October 25, 2006, pp. 5, 19, 23; archived at http://www.bmvg.de/portal/PA_1_0_LT/PortalFiles/C1256EF4003 6B05B/W26UWAMT995INFOEN/WB+2006+englisch+DS.pdf?y w_repository=youatweb.

[111] BMZ, *Observations on Service Delivery in Fragile States and Situations: The German Perspective*, Berlin: April 12, 2006, http://www.bmz.de/en/service/infothek/fach/spezial/spezial145/Sp ecial145.pdf.

[112] Adolf Klocke-Lesch, "German Development Policy on States at Risk and State-Building," Berlin: BMZ, January 2004, archived at http://www.oecd.org/dataoecd/30/44/34242695.pdf. BMZ, *BMZ Discourse on Development-Based and Military Responses to the New Security Challenges*, May 2004.

[113] BMZ, "Sector Strategy for Crisis Prevention, Conflict Transformation, and Peace-Building in German Development Cooperation," Berlin: June 2005. To support BMZ's work on conflict, GTZ has launched a Program for Crisis Prevention and Conflict Transformation.

[114] *Civilian Crisis Prevention, Conflict Resolution and Post-Conflict Reconstruction*, Berlin: Die Bundesregierung, May 12, 2004.

[115] The first of these reports, released in May 2006, places Germany's national efforts in the context of three reference documents: the ESS; the European Consensus on Development Cooperation; and the UN Secretary-General's Report *In Larger Freedom*. See *Working Together to Strengthen Security and Stability through Crisis Prevention*, First Federal Government Report on Implementation of the Action Plan, Berlin: Die Bundesregierung, May 2006.

[116] An advisory board composed of representatives from the research, NGO, and private sector communities has been established to provide input to the Action Plan, but its role has been marginal.

[117] Among other tasks, according to the Action Plan, the Steering

Group is supposed to partner with parliamentarians, civil society, the private sector and academia; promote country or regional strategies; facilitate interministerial consultations; advise and support ministries on crisis prevention concepts; help ensure the shift from early warning to early action; coordinate with distinct bodies of the Federal Government dealing with crisis prevention; and develop models and processes to draw at short notice on the crisis prevention capacities of ministries. *Civilian Crisis Prevention, Conflict Resolution and Post-Conflict Reconstruction*, p. 101.

[118] In the previous coalition, the Green Party was the primary champion of this issue, supported by the Social Democratic Party (SPD). In the current government, the Greens are out, and the SPD-led Foreign Ministry and BMZ have lost power relative to the Chancellor's Office, the MoD, and the Economics Ministry, which are more skeptical.

[119] *Working Together to Strengthen Security and Stability through Crisis Prevention*, Berlin, 2006.

[120] There has been some effort to second staff from one agency to another, in a move to bridge cultures.

[121] BMZ also maintains a Peace Fund to support local efforts for violent conflict management and peacebuilding.

[122] *Shared Responsibility: Sweden's Policy for Global Development*, Government Bill 2002/03:122. Sweden is among the most generous providers of ODA, devoting some one percent of its GDP to this purpose.

[123] *Project on Fragile States: Final Report*, Policy Analysis Office, Swedish Ministry of Foreign Affairs, 2005, available at http://www.regeringen.se/content/1/c6/06/12/71/c7b3bc13.pdf. Robert Picciotto, 'Funmi Olonisakin, and Michael Clarke, *Global Development and Human Security: Towards a Policy Agenda*, a policy review commissioned by the Ministry of Foreign Affairs, Sweden, London: 2005, available at http://www.egdi.gov.se/pdf/global_development_human_security.pdf.

[124] *Project on Fragile States, Final Report*, p. 29.

[125] http://www.oecd.org/document/46/0,2340,en_2649_33693550_35233262_1_1_1_1,00.html.

[126] Swedish Government Bill 2004/05:5, *Our Future Defence: The Focus of Swedish Defence Policy 2005-2007*, available at http://www.sweden.gov.se/content/1/c6/03/21/19/224a4b3c.pdf.

[127] SIDA, *Promoting Peace and Security through Development Cooperation* (Stockholm: SIDA, October 1, 2005).

[128] Ministry of Foreign Affairs, Sweden, *Guidelines for Cooperation Strategies* (Stockholm, 2005).

[129] OECD, *DAC Peer Review: Main Findings and Recommendations, Sweden*

(2005), available at
http://www.oecd.org/document/15/0,2340,en_2649_34603_34950
223_1_1_1_1,00.html.

130 While SIDA does have some flexible contingency funds, it is not considered legitimate for the Foreign Minister to try to force a shift or reallocation of funding, even in crisis situations.

131 Swedish Government Bill, 2004/05:5, *Our Future Defence.*

132 The MoD looks to the EU as the main forum for Sweden's contribution to peace support operations, such as Operation Artemis in the Democratic Republic of Congo under French leadership.

133 Government Offices, Ministry for Foreign Affairs, "Riktlinjer for svensk hallning gentemot Sudan," Stockholm: May 5, 2004.

134 Even here, one finds tensions within development agencies over whether to focus on "fragility" or on "conflict," two phenomena that overlap but are not identical.

135 When they do invoke "fragility," they tend to apply the term to a wider range of developing countries where instability, violence, or state failure may have negative spillover effects for the national security of rich countries.

136 The Netherlands and Norway, although not covered in this study, provide cases in point.

137 This may not always be possible in countries like Germany, where departments are constitutionally sovereign. In countries with a strongly consensual political culture, like Sweden, such firm direction may be unnecessary.

138 A critical question is whether such units will attempt to undertake the full panoply of potential roles—including training and capacity building, planning and directing actual missions, and deploying personnel to the field—or simply a subset of these.

139 Robert Picciotto, et al., *Striking a New Balance.*

140 One of the main impediments to such coherence is that ambassadors tend to be focused on diplomatic and security concerns, and often lack familiarity with development principles and practice.

141 Lisa Chauvet and Paul Collier, "Helping Hand? Aid to Failing States," June 2006, available at http://users.ox.ac.uk/~econpco/research/pdfs/HelpingHand-AidtoFailingStates.pdf. Levin and Dollar, "The Forgotten States. "Low Income Countries Under Stress: Update," World Bank Operations Policy and Country Services, December 1, 2005, available at http://www-wds.worldbank.org/servlet/WDSContentServer/WDSP/IB/2005/12/22/000090341_20051222092710/Rendered/PDF/34789.pdf. OECD/DAC, Principles for Good International Engagement in Fragile States, April 7, 2005, available at http://www.oecd.org/dataoecd/59/55/34700989.pdf. World Bank,

"Making Aid Work in Fragile States: Case Studies of Effective Aid-Financed Programs," World Bank Background Document, 2004, available at http://www.oecd.org/dataoecd/31/63/34252765.pdf.

[142] OECD/DAC, *Monitoring Resource Flows to Fragile States*, DAC News, July 26, 2006, available at http://www.oecd.org/dataoecd/48/6/37046754.htm.

About the Authors

Stewart Patrick is a Research Fellow at the Center for Global Development and a Professorial Lecturer at the School of Advanced International Studies of Johns Hopkins University. He joined CGD from the Secretary of State's Policy Planning Staff, where he helped formulate US policy on Afghanistan as well as a range of global and transnational challenges. Dr. Patrick is a current member and former international affairs fellow of the Council on Foreign Relations. Previously, he was research associate at the Center on International Cooperation at New York University. Among other writings, he is co-author and co-editor of *Multilateralism and US Foreign Policy: Ambivalent Engagement*, and *Good Intentions: Pledges of Aid for Post-Conflict Recovery*.

Kaysie Brown is a Program Associate at the Center for Global Development, where she studies fragile states. Before joining CGD, she was a senior program officer at the International Peace Academy in New York, where her research focused on natural resources and conflict, security sector reform, and rule of law efforts in peace operations. Ms. Brown has published numerous articles on topics such as legacies of war economies in post-conflict peacebuilding, police reform in the South Pacific, and rule of law initiatives in UN peace operations. She received her Masters degree from Oxford University.